IN LOYAL REMEMBRANCE
OF
ROBERT THE BRUCE
KING OF SCOTS
WHOSE VICTORY IN THIS
GLEN OVER AN ENGLISH
FORCE IN MARCH 1307
OPENED THE CAMPAIGN OF
INDEPENDENCE WHICH HE
BROUGHT TO A DECISIVE
CLOSE AT BANNOCKBURN
ON 24TH JUNE 1314.

Scotland

100 Legendary Places

ROUGH GUIDES

Scotland

100 Legendary Places

Scotland
100 Legendary Places

EDINBURGH & THE LOTHIANS

THE BORDERS

DUMFRIES & GALLOWAY

AYRSHIRE & ARRAN

GLASGOW & THE CLYDE

ARGYLL & BUTE

STIRLING, LOCH LOMOND & THE TROSSACHS

FIFE

Introduction

Scotland is a country where legend sits noticeably close to everyday life. You can see it in the names on the signposts or the sudden outline of a castle above a town, not to mention the way that the weather can turn a coastline theatrical in minutes.

For many visitors, Edinburgh is the nation's first great impression, poised beneath its crag and busy with festivals. But each city tells its own story: Glasgow's music and museums, Dundee's waterfront reinvention, Aberdeen's granite glint. Beyond the cities, small harbours and market towns deliver their own rewards, from a lobster shack on the East Neuk to a cobbled lane that seems to have misplaced the present day.

Out of town, dramatic and expressive landscapes take over. Highland glens open into wide moorland, lochs thread between hills, and long roads lead to beaches that look almost tropical when the light behaves. Offshore, islands pull you further into something otherworldly – whisky-scented shores, machair meadows, sea cliffs loud with birds, and communities that maintain their own rhythms.

The 100 legendary places in these pages have been chosen for the moments they spark, from a viewpoint earned to a quiet chapel or a stone circle at dusk, or a pub fire after rain. Follow the famous highlights, then take the detour. Scotland is generous with surprises at the next bend.

MACKINTOSH
AT THE
WILLOW

V&A

Edinburgh & THE Lothians

Edinburgh can feel like something of a stage set built from rock, smoke and legend. Spires and stone stairways lead to sudden views, and pockets of quiet can be found just a lane away from the crowds. Days begin with sea-bright air from the Firth of Forth and end in warm lamplight, with music drifting from pubs and festival tents. Beyond the city, in the Lothians, soft farmland and ancient ruins bring space, silence and a hint of the uncanny.

Arthur's Seat

You don't often find an ancient volcano looming above a city, but Arthur's Seat is exactly that: a 823ft rocky hulk crouched over Edinburgh like a lion. Hiking to the summit is a much-loved pastime for weekending urban folk; it's a steep climb, but perfectly doable with a decent level of fitness. The rewards: phenomenal views of the Old and New towns, Edinburgh Castle and the glinting Firth of Forth. At the foot of the hill sits the dramatic and unusual Scottish Parliament building: Spanish architect Enric Miralles designed a blueprint with windows framing the peak to give the politicians, quite literally, loftier and more inspiring views. Once you've caught your breath, trace the rough paths and stone steps to the long line of the Salisbury Crags, from where a paved track descends to Holyrood.

(L) The walk down from Arthur's Seat

Duddingston

Tucked into the lee of Arthur's Seat on the edge of a nature reserve, the sleepy village of Duddingston is a world apart from Edinburgh. The whole place – all two streets' worth – quietly marinates in Scottish history, with the Sheep Heid Inn laying fair claim to oldest pub (est. 1360) in the land. The clientele has included Mary, Queen of Scots, King James I and Bonnie Prince Charlie, with the latter holding a council of war just down the street at no. 8–10. Parallel to The Causeway is Old Church Lane, where a revelation of a secret garden lies sequestered behind high stone walls. Brought to life in the 1960s by husband-and-wife GPs, Dr Neil's Garden is a little slice of horticultural paradise filled with exotic trees and plants. Beguiling paths wend their way past Scots pine, Chilean araucaria (AKA monkey puzzle) and American sequoia down to the edge of Duddingston Loch, populated by herons, kingfishers and otters. Even in summer, the garden is rarely busy and you can sometimes have it all to yourself. When the sun shines and the light blinks off the water, you might be anywhere but rain-lashed Scotland.

(L) Herons, kingfishers and otters populate Duddingston Loch; (T) Duddingston Allotments; (B) Old Church Lane

Edinburgh Old Town

(T) Edinburgh Old Town from Calton Hill

Edinburgh's medieval Old Town, only about a mile long and 400yds wide, is the evocative heart of the historic city, with its tenements, courtyards, ghosts and catacombs cheek-by-jowl with many of Scotland's most important buildings. In addition to the obvious attractions of the Castle and the Holyrood at either end of the famous Royal Mile, you'll find a feast of architecture styles along the length and breadth of the street. In the past decade, the city's culinary scene has surged in style and sophistication thanks to inventive chefs reimagining traditional Scottish food at the likes of Wedgwood, Ondine and La Garrigue. Despite its tourist trappings, the Old Town is a hub of daily business conducted in the law courts, city chambers and, of course, Scottish Parliament – housed in a radical and controversial set of buildings. For unforgettable vistas, head to Calton Hill to see the spire-studded skyline unfurl before you.

Jupiter Artland

Combining the best of contemporary and landscape art with the bucolic charms of a working country estate, Jupiter Artland makes for a unique day-trip from Edinburgh. The brainchild of an art-collecting couple, the sculpture park sits in the 100-acre grounds of Bonnington House, 10 miles from the capital. Admirers of the late landscape designer Charles Jencks will instantly clock his trademark biospheric mounds at the entrance: the pristinely sculpted, cascading *Cells of Life* that flank the lake-dotted causeway. You likewise can't fail to miss Joana Vasconcelos' *Gateway*, a kaleidoscopic swimming pool made from over eleven thousand Portuguese tiles. Explore more and you might discover Andy Goldsworthy's *Coppice Room* and its conspiratorial huddle of trees, or the darkly humorous, dystopian funhouse of Rachel Maclean's *Mimi*. The gorgeous Jacobean interiors of the galleries are as much as of a draw as the exhibitions.

(O) Joana Vasconcelos' 'Gateway'; (L) Rachel Maclean's 'Mimi'; (T) 'Animitasa' by Christian Boltanski

Linlithgow Palace

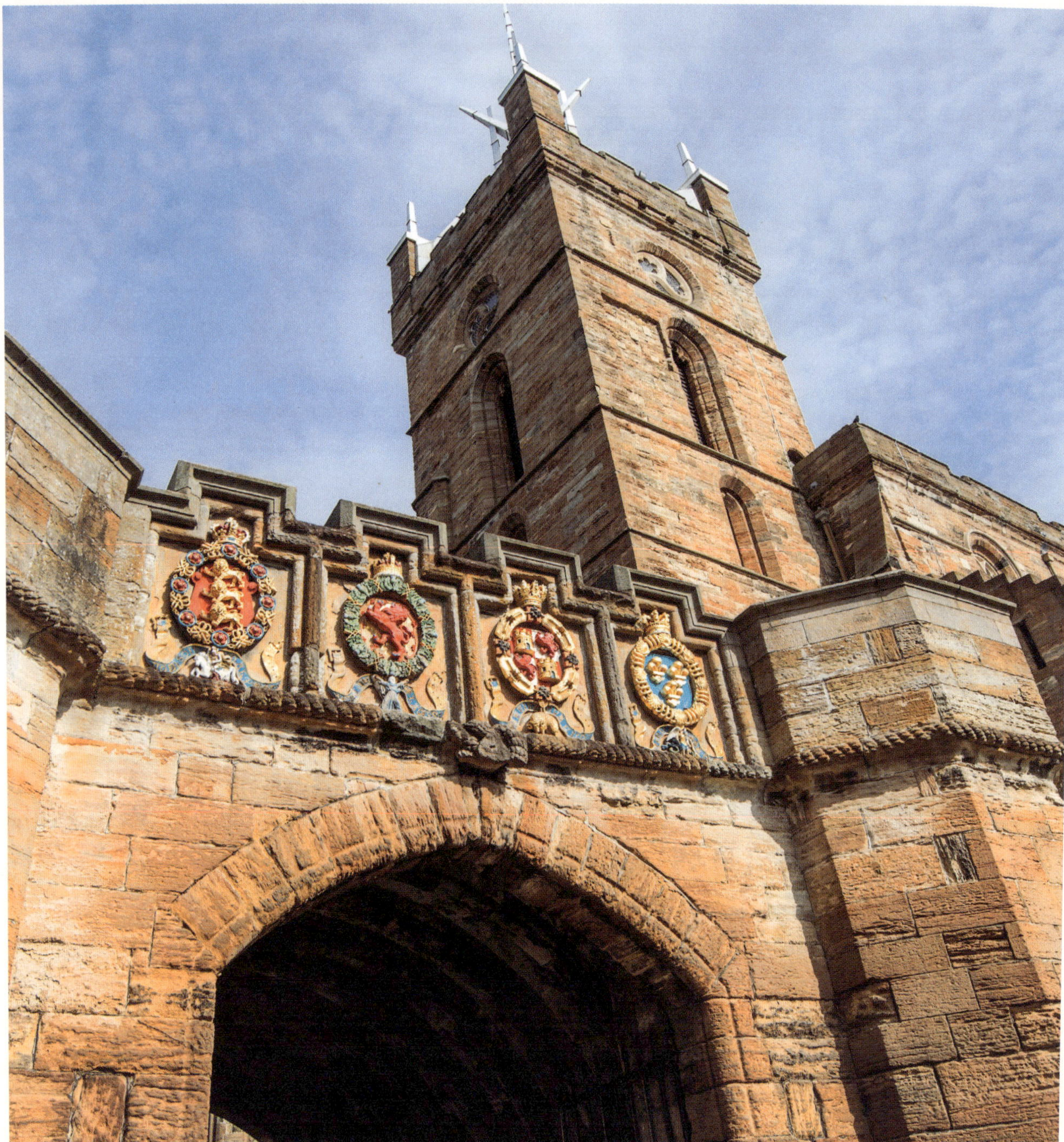

Linlithgow Palace is a splendid fifteenth-century ruin romantically set on the edge of Linlithgow Loch. The pile is associated with some of Scotland's best-known historical figures, including Mary, Queen of Scots, who was born here on December 8, 1542 and became queen six days later. A royal manor house is believed to have existed on this site since the time of David I, though James I began construction of the present palace, a process that continued through two centuries and the reign of no fewer than eight monarchs. From the top of the northwest tower, Queen Margaret looked out in vain for the return of James IV from the field of Flodden in 1513 – indeed, the views from her bower, six giddy storeys up from the ground, are exceptional. The ornate octagonal fountain in the inner courtyard, with its wonderfully intricate figures and medallion heads, flowed with wine for the wedding of James V and Mary of Guise. The galleried Great Hall is magnificent, as is the adjoining kitchen.

(L) Grand entrance to Linlithgow Palace; (T) Linlithgow Palace at dusk; (B) The Palace and St Michael's church from above

National Museum of Scotland

The National Museum of Scotland sits at the heart of Edinburgh, and is very much a place of two halves. There's a fantastical Victorian wing that packs in a bedazzling array of artefacts, covering natural history, world culture, geology and technology. One standout exhibit is the gruesome Millennium Clock Tower, a jumble of cogs, chains and wheels modelled in the form of a Gothic cathedral, with gargoyles and sinister-looking figurines representing characters from twentieth-century politics. The newer building – a bold sandstone addition fronted by a striking cylindrical tower – traces Scotland's history, from the earliest people to the Union of the Crowns, the Jacobite Rebellion, the Industrial Revolution and on to pop culture and contemporary politics. Key exhibits are the quirkily expressive Lewis chessmen, a silver picnic set made for Bonnie Prince Charlie and a life-size working model of a steam-driven Newcomen Atmospheric Engine.

(O) The fantastical Victorian Wing; (L) Life-sized skeleton of a Tyrannosaurus rex; (T) World Cultures gallery; (B) The cylindrical tower of the new wing

Rosslyn Chapel

Sitting in hilly Midlothian south of Edinburgh, the fifteenth-century Rosslyn Chapel is revered for its sublime stone carvings – some of the finest in the world – and the subject of intrigue and mystery with its alleged Crusader connections. This richly decorated cathedral-like Gothic masterpiece is a testament to the skills of its medieval sculptors. Built in a highly ornate style, its exterior is a riot of flying buttresses, pinnacles and leering gargoyles – but it is the interior that fascinates with its stories etched in stone. First up, there are depictions of cacti and Indian corn that predate Columbus's 'discovery' of America. Secondly, there's the intricately knotted Apprentice Pillar, a work so dazzling that the jealous master allegedly killed his apprentice, whose figure – complete with violently slashed head – is scored into the ceiling. Thirdly, there are the Freemason and Knights Templar associations, signalled by carvings of a floriated cross and a five-point star, that have sparked the myth that the chapel houses the Holy Grail.

(L) Exterior cross window; (T) View into the nave vault; (B) The exterior

Edinburgh Castle

If Edinburgh is Scotland's calling card, the Castle is the signature – a brute of stone crouched on its volcanic plug, visible from half the city and stamped on a thousand postcards for good reason. The approach alone, up through the Old Town's closes and courtyards, feels like climbing into history: kings and rebels, sieges and swagger, all compressed into a skyline of battlements. Inside, the drama keeps coming, from cavernous halls to viewpoints that make sense of Edinburgh's split personality – medieval Old Town, poised New Town, and the steel-grey glint of the Forth beyond. Come early or late if you can, when the esplanade quietens and the Castle returns to what it does best: brooding over the capital like it owns it.

(L) Edinburgh Castle from Blackford Hill

THE Borders

Tucked between the Cheviots and the Lammermuirs, the Borders is a land of green river valleys, rounded hills and big skies, where ancient abbeys brood above the Tweed and market towns hum with rugby pride. Walk woodland trails, trace clifftops above seabird colonies, and follow quiet lanes past stately homes. History here is lived as well as visited, present in proud traditions and local identity – and around every river bend there's a new, quietly stirring scene.

Glentress Forest

(T) Biking the cycle paths of Glentress Forest

Glentress Forest has some of the best opportunities for mountain biking in Scotland. Not only are there five superb, carefully crafted, purpose-built trails – colour-coded for difficulty – there's a fantastic bike centre at the entrance to the forest called the Peel Gateway. This is a great place for bikers, with changing rooms and showers, a café and a shop filled with spares as well as bike rental from Alpine Bikes. If you fancy staying several days it's worth checking out the timber wigwams of Glentress Forest Lodges near the entrance. There are more adrenaline-pumping downhill trails through thick forest just a few miles southeast of Glentress near Innerleithen, geared towards more advanced riders, with bike rental available in Innerleithen. Glentress and Innerleithen combined are one of seven forest biking centres in southern Scotland, known collectively as the 7stanes.

Jedburgh Abbey

Founded in the twelfth century as an Augustinian priory by King David I, Jedburgh Abbey is the best preserved of all the Border abbeys. The abbey was burnt and badly damaged on several occasions, but by far the worst destruction was inflicted by the English in the 1540s. By this time, the contemplative way of life had already fallen prey to corruption and only a few canons remained living in the abbey ruins, until it was closed in 1560. All that survives are the foundations and basic ground plan. The Abbey Church, however, remained the parish kirk for another three centuries, so is particularly intact and splendidly preserved. As you enter via the west door, the three-storey nave's parade of columns and arches lies before you, a fine example of the transition from Romanesque to Gothic design, with pointed window arches surmounted by the round-headed arches of the triforium, which, in turn, support the lancet windows of the clerestory. Climb the narrow staircase to the balcony, where you can imagine how the place must have looked decked out for the 1285 marriage of Alexander III to Yolande de Dreux.

(L) The arches in the ruins of Jedburgh Abbey; (T) Jedburgh is the best preserved of all the Border abbeys; (B) A fine example of the transition from Romanesque to Gothic design

Melrose

Tucked in between the River Tweed and Eildon Hills, Melrose is one of the most appealing towns in the Borders. Centred around a busy little market square, its narrow streets are trimmed by a harmonious ensemble of styles, from quaint cottages and shops to tall Georgian and Victorian facades. The forest scenery inspired Sir Walter Scott, whose own home, Abbotsford, lies a few miles outside town. As the birthplace in 1883 of the Rugby Sevens, Melrose swarms during Sevens Week in April and the Borders Book Festival in June. The town's chief draw is its Abbey, dating from 1136. Legend has it that the heart of Robert I is buried here (his body rests at Dunfermline Abbey). The site is dominated by the Abbey Church, which has lost its west front, and whose nave today consists of the window arches and chapels of the south aisle. The sculptural detail is extraordinary: columns etched with curly kale carving; facades scored with figures holding scrolls bearing inscriptions such as "He suffered because he willed it". There's also the Trimontium Museum, a treasure chest of Roman artefacts. Nearby, Leaderfoot Viaduct reaches over the Tweed, 126ft above the river valley. Dating back to 1863, the disused railway is one of the area's most striking landmarks.

(O) Abbotsford gardens; (L) Melrose is lined with characterful cafés; (T) Borders Book Festival hits the town in June; (B) The Abbey

Traquair House

Peeping out from the trees just south of Innerleithen, Traquair House is the oldest continuously inhabited house in Scotland, with the present line of owners – the Maxwell Stuarts – having lived here since 1491. The first laird of Traquair inherited a fortified tower, which his powerful descendants converted into a mansion that was visited, it is said, by 27 monarchs, including Mary, Queen of Scots. The whitewashed facade is strikingly handsome, with narrow window, trim turrets and a dinky front door. Inside, original vaulted cellars once hid locals' cattle away from raiders, and the twisting staircase provided a secret escape route for persecuted Catholics until the Emancipation Act in 1829. Museum treasures include a rosary and crucifix owned by Mary, Queen of Scots and the cloak worn by the Earl of Nithsdale during his dramatic escape from the Tower of London, where he was under sentence of death for his part in the Jacobite Rising of 1715. The earl was saved by his wife who got his jailers drunk and smuggled him out disguised as a maid in spite of his red beard. Tackle the maze then reward your efforts in the Traquair House Brewery, which dates back to 1566. When you leave, dodge the Bear Gates; Bonnie Prince Charlie left the house through the gates, and the then-owner promised to keep them locked until a Stuart should ascend the throne.

(L) Traquair House's entrance

St Abb's Head

Scotland's southeast doesn't do showy peaks, but it delivers cliff drama with a sharp, salty edge – and St Abb's Head is where it all comes together. The path threads through tough coastal grassland and heather before the land drops away into a sudden amphitheatre of rock, sea and sky. In season, the cliffs are alive with seabirds, and the air has that unmistakable tang of guano and spray that marks a proper breeding colony. St Abb's Head is particularly seductive thanks to its beguiling combination of scale and intimacy. One minute you're watching waves hammer the stacks as far as the eye can see, the next you're close enough to hear the rasp and chatter from the ledges. Even on a calm day, it feels wild, like the North Sea is just waiting to change its mind.

(L) View towards St Abbs from St Abb's Head; (T) Sunset at Pettico Wick;
(B) Northern gannets, common guillemots and razorbills

Dumfries & Galloway

Scotland's southwest corner feels like a secret detour off the motorway: wide, empty hills, dark forests and a soft-edged coast of sandy coves and saltmarsh. Dumfries and Galloway mixes ruined abbeys and moated castles with the 'Scottish Riviera' glow of the Solway, where warm light lingers on red sandstone and seabirds. Inland, quiet lanes lead to garden surprises and star-filled skies above the brooding Galloway Hills.

Caerlaverock Castle

Picture-perfect Caerlaverock Castle, a moated ruin, was built in the late thirteenth century out of the rich local red sandstone. It is unique for being one of the very few triangular fortresses in the world; indeed, during the siege of 1300 by Edward I, a contemporary bard commented: "In shape it was like a shield, for it had but three sides round it, with a tower at each corner." Caerlaverock sustained further damage in 1312, this time from the Scots, and again in 1356–57 from the English, forcing numerous rebuilds. Beyond the mighty double-towered gatehouse, you're confronted by the ornate Renaissance facade of the Nithsdale Lodging, erected in the 1630s by the first Earl of Nithsdale, Robert Maxwell. Just six years later the earl and his garrison were forced to surrender after a thirteen-week siege by the Covenanters, who proceeded to wreck the place. It was never inhabited again. The facade retains exquisite architectural detail, not least the various coat-of-arms and allegorical scenes above each window; look out for Neptune being drawn by a sea creature in a chariot.

(L) One of the few triangular fortresses in the world

Galloway Forest Park

Britain's largest forest and first Dark Sky Park, Galloway Forest Park stretches 774 square kilometres across the Galloway glens and hills. The park has three visitor centres with graded walking trails that crisscross the peaceful woodland; Kirroughtree and Glentrool also have excellent mountain-biking facilities with trailheads and bike hire. The third, Clatteringshaws has a lovely lochside café and is an easy stroll to the granite stone where Robert the Bruce is said to have rested after victory against the English in 1307. From here, follow the Gariland Burn to Loch Neldricken and Loch Enoch, with their silver granite sands, and then on to the Devil's Bowling Green, strewn with hundreds of erratic boulders left by the retreating glaciers. Potential wildlife sightings in the park include red squirrels, red deer and the back-from-near-extinction red kite. The Raiders' Road, a 16km route tracing the River Dee, is a scenic drive dotted with waterfalls and natural pools where you can swim. Thanks to a lack of light pollution, the park offers out-of-this-world stargazing; the finest locations include the visitor centres and lochs.

(L) The Southern Upland Way; (T) Loch Trool; (B) Britain's first Dark Sky Park is perfect for stargazing

THE Garden *OF* Cosmic Speculation

There aren't many gardens that could live up to such a grandiloquent title but Charles Jencks' masterpiece fits the bill. The fact that public access is limited to one day a year only adds to the allure. Across thirty acres of Dumfriesshire countryside, the late doyen of landscape design translated his "cosmic" goal of finding relationships between the big and small, science and spirituality, the universe and the landscape. Trademark contoured mounds echo prehistoric barrows, Incan terraces and the Nazca Lines, while evoking the mindbending infinity of fractals. The Black Hole Terrace deepens the optical illusion, warping time and space with its chequerboard of Astroturf and metal sheeting, accompanied by a metallic double helix. Elsewhere, sculpted and bisected pools recall both the earth's oceanic beginnings and the causeways of ancient Mexico.

(L) The Snail Mound; (C) DNA double helix in the Physic Garden; (R) The Jumping Bridge

Kirkcudbright

(T) View over the town

A handsome little harbour town of broad streets and brightly painted houses, Kirkcudbright ("kir-coo-bree") has long been a favoured haunt for artists and painters, none more so than the revered "Glasgow Boys", who sought inspiration in its unique combination of light and landscape. One such artist was Edward Hornel (an associate of the Glasgow Boys), whose life and work you can admire at Broughton House where he resided between 1901 and his death in 1933; these days, his old studio is given over to an artist in residence. For an overview of these chaps, as well as some of Scotland's other famous artists, pop into the shiny Kirkcudbright Galleries. The town also rates a clutch of other eminently appealing sites, from the sturdy MacLellan's Castle to one of the most haphazardly enjoyable collections you'll find anywhere, courtesy of the Stewartry Museum, which holds objects as diverse as clay pipes and pickled fish.

MULL OF GALLOWAY
WIGTOWNSHIRE
LAND'S END 318 MILES
DOUGLAS 37 MILES
JOHN O'G
OATS 285 MILES
BELFAST 42 MILES
LONDON 293 MILES
SENEGAL - OUR GANNETS' WINTER HOME 2800 MILES

Rhins of Galloway

For a real sense of perspective, few trips in Scotland beat the contemplative quiet of the Rhins of Galloway. The country's southernmost point, the hammer-headed peninsula is visible from afar and along the coast thanks to the chess piece-style Mull of Galloway Lighthouse. The sense of remoteness is palpable, whether you're taking a cliff walk to the foghorn and viewing platform overlooking the 260ft-high cliffs, or visiting the RSPB visitor centre to loop through the bird-nested heathland. Climb the 115 steps to the top of the lighthouse for epic vistas, or go for a bracing dip on one of the sandy beaches lacing the peninsula. Some of the finest strands are the coves beside the harbour town of Portpatrick and those wrapping around Victorian-era Knockinaam Lodge, where Sir Winston Churchill plotted D-Day from his favourite hotel room.

(L) Mull of Galloway Lighthouse; (T) The hammer-headed peninsula anchors southwest Scotland; (B) The sandy beach at Portpatrick

Wigtown

What Hay-on-Wye is to Wales, Wigtown is to Scotland. As pleasant as it is, Wigtown wouldn't ordinarily merit any special kind of visit were it not for the fact that it boasts around a dozen bookshops lining either side of its high street. Most offer a general selection of titles – mainly secondhand – but there are plenty of specialist shops too, such as Byre Books, which focuses on film, theatre and television, and the wonderfully titled Foggie Toddle, whose speciality is children's books. But the town really comes into its own at the end of September during the annual Wigtown Book Festival. A wonderful programme of literary events, including readings and performance art, takes place in bookshops, a central marquee on the main square, and several other outdoor venues. There's invariably a stellar line-up too, with past authors including Val McDermid and Louis de Bernières.

(O) The Open Book; (L) Byre Books specializes in media titles; (T) The Book Shop: does what it says on the tin; (B) Vintage tomes in The Book Shop

Ayrshire & Arran

Rolling farmland and big horizons characterize Ayrshire's rural landscape, framed by broad sandy beaches offering bracing sea walks, adjacent to world-class golf. Inland, dive into layers of heritage in stately homes, cliff-edge castles and villages steeped in Robert Burns, while out in the Firth of Clyde, island silhouettes hover on the horizon. Chief among them is Arran, rising like "Scotland in miniature", with whisky, wildlife and big views in every direction.

Ailsa Craig

(T) View towards Ailsa Craig

As you travel along the South Ayrshire coast, the giant muffin-shaped island of Ailsa Craig looms on the horizon, stranded as it is in the middle of the Firth of Clyde. The island's name means "Fairy Rock" in Gaelic, though it was a less than enchanting place for the persecuted Catholics who escaped here during the Reformation. The island's granite has long been used for making what many consider to be the finest curling stones – a company in nearby Mauchline still has exclusive rights to gather the boulders. In the late nineteenth century, 29 people lived on the island, working in the quarry or at the Stevenson lighthouse. With its volcanic, columnar cliffs and 1114ft summit, Ailsa Craig is now a bird sanctuary that's home to some 40,000 gannets, plus thousands of other seabirds. Visit at the end of May and in June to see the fledglings trying to fly. Trips to the island depart from Girvan, 21 miles south of Ayr, and take about an hour, after which you get enough time to walk up to the summit and watch the birds.

Arran

Shaped like a kidney bean and occupying centre stage in the Firth of Clyde, Arran is the most southerly of all the Scottish islands. The Highland–Lowland dividing line passes right through its centre – hence the cliché about it being like "Scotland in miniature" – leaving the northern half sparsely populated, mountainous and bleak, while the lush southern half enjoys a milder climate. There are two big crowd-pullers on Arran: geology and golf. The former has fascinated rock-obsessed students since Sir James Hutton came here in the late eighteenth century to confirm his theories of uniformitarianism, and it's still a popular field trip destination today. A hundred years later, Sir Archibald Geikie's investigations were a landmark in the study of Arran's geology. As for golf, Arran boasts seven courses, including three of the eighteen-hole variety at Brodick, Lamlash and Whiting Bay, and a unique twelve-hole course at Shiskine, near Blackwaterfoot.

(O) Houses cluster on the shore of Lamlash Bay below Goat Fell, the island's highest peak; (L) The fairy pools of Glen Rosa; (T) A riot of colourful wildflowers in spring

Burns Trail

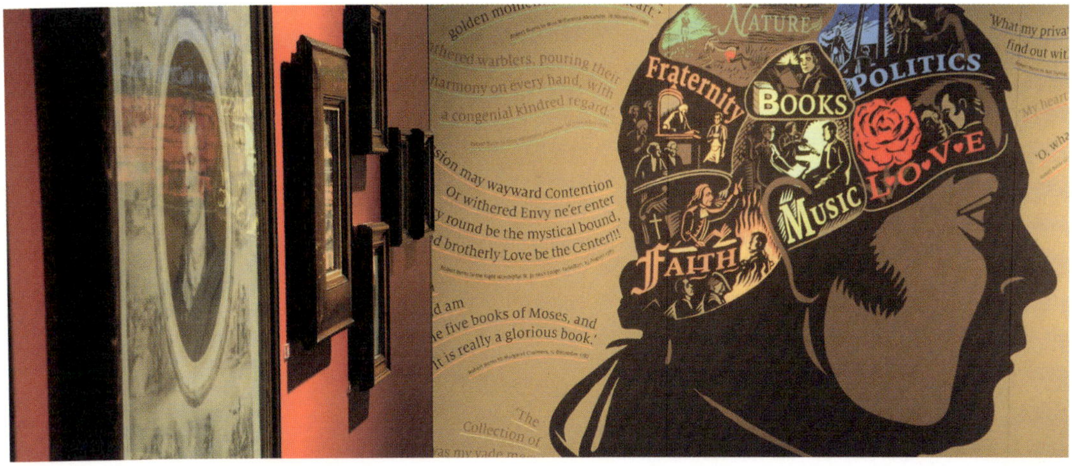

Radical, romantic, rampant womanizer and, above all, genius poet of the Scots tongue, Robert Burns was born in the village of Alloway in Ayrshire. If you'd like to find out more about the writer of such vigorous, life-affirming songs and verses as *Tam o' Shanter*, *Auld Lang Syne* and *Green Grow the Rushes, O*, then this is the place to start. Burns Cottage is the whitewashed home built by the poet's father, William, to house his family: they lived in one room with the animals next door. The nearby Burns Birthplace Museum is packed with memorabilia, including the pistol Burns used as an exciseman. Other sites on the local Burns Trail include the roofless ruins of Alloway Auld Kirk where drunken Tam encountered dancing witches, and Brig o' Doon, the hump-backed bridge over which Tam was chased on horseback by his supernatural foes. Six miles north of Alloway is The Bachelors' Club in Tarbolton, where the twenty-year-old Burns danced, and set up a debating club.

(L) Brig o' Doon; (T) Explore the Mind of Robert Burns exhibition; (B) Burns Cottage, built by the poet's father

Culzean Castle

In a country that has more than its fair share of heart-pounding castles, it takes something special to take your breath away. Though it is conceived with the same baronial grace as so many in the Highlands, Culzean Castle steals the show thanks to its awe-inspiring location. From its cliff-hugging perch above sculpted coves that recast the sun-drowsy Ayrshire coast as the Adriatic, the turreted sixteenth-century abode appears as though it was built on top of the crashing Atlantic waves. Guides will tell you that the castle made a lasting impression on former US President Eisenhower when he stayed here while in office, but more fantastic are the rumours that seven ghosts haunt the corridors. Instead of spectres and ghouls, just hope you only find creaky stairways and stories of the lords and ladies who once lived here. The grounds – a riot of colour in summer – are filled with twisted woods, secret follies, a walled garden, an ice house, clock tower, deer park and swan pond.

(O) Fountain-dotted gardens; (L) Seven ghosts are rumoured to haunt the corridors; (T) Fans of the castle include former US President Eisenhower; (B) Deer Park

Dumfries House

A handsome Palladian villa, Dumfries House was commissioned by the fifth Earl of Dumfries, a widower who wanted to remarry and ensure that he had an heir for the family estate. The house, the first major early commission for the Adam brothers, was conceived as a honey trap to lure a potential wife, and, judging by the portrait of the ageing, gouty earl in the Pink Drawing Room, he needed all the help he could get. Such was the earl's urgency, the house was built and decked out swiftly – between 1756 and 1760 – meaning its Rococo decor is in perfect harmony with the graceful sandstone exterior. The earl secured a wife but died without producing an heir; the family subsequently turned their attention to creating Mount Stuart, leaving Dumfries House to be looked after by a series of housekeepers. The recent story of the house is as remarkable as its past: the building and its contents were all up for sale in 2007, and some of the furniture had begun its journey south to Christie's when the then-Prince Charles and a hastily assembled trust intervened to make a heritage "save". Chief among the treasures is an outstanding collection of Chippendale furniture, including a truly spectacular, one-of-a-kind rosewood bookcase, reputedly now worth around £20 million.

(L) Dumfries House was commissioned by the fifth Earl of Dumfries

Glasgow & THE Clyde

Glasgow hits with a rush of energy, leading with bold architecture, quick wit and a lived-in grit that only sharpens its charm. Museums and galleries spill with imagination, music venues keep the nights busy, and the city's design pedigree shows in everything from Art Nouveau flourishes to modern waterfront reinvention. Follow the River Clyde beyond the centre and the mood shifts to day-trip ease – from old shipbuilding shores to green valleys made for slow walks.

Clydeside

CLYDEPORT
EAT
DRINK
ENJOY
RELAX
CITY
CAFé
RIVERSIDE
BEER GARDEN
AL FRESCO
DINING

"The Clyde made Glasgow and Glasgow made the Clyde" runs an old saw, full of sentimentality for the days when the river was the world's premier shipbuilding centre, and when its industry lent a confidence that made Glasgow the second city of the British Empire. The last of the great liners to be built on Clydeside was the QE2 in 1967, yet such events are hard to visualize today. The banks of the river are all but devoid of any industry: shipbuilding is now restricted to a couple of yards. Following a flurry of construction in recent years, however, Clydeside has once again become a focus of attention. Striking constructions such as the titanium-clad SEC Armadillo auditorium, the creatively lit Clyde Arc and the enormous SSE HydroGlasgow: centre have become icons of the city's forward-thinking image. On the opposite side stands the box-like home of BBC Scotland and the curvaceous Glasgow Science Centre. Its shipbuilding heritage has not been forgotten though, with the Tall Ship Glenlee, located next to the superb Riverside Museum, and the Finnieston Crane retained as an icon of shipbuilding days.

(L) Finnieston Crane; (T) Riverside Museum; (B) Glasgow Science Centre

Necropolis

Rising up behind the cathedral, the atmospheric Necropolis is a grassy mound covered in a fantastic assortment of crumbling and tumbling gravestones, ornate urns, gloomy catacombs and Neoclassical temples. Inspired by the Père Lachaise cemetery in Paris, this garden of death was established in 1832, and it quickly became a fitting spot for the great and the good of wealthy nineteenth-century Glasgow to indulge their vanity; some 50,000 burials have taken place since the first one, and there are 3,500 monuments. Various paths lead through the rows of eroding, neglected graves, and from the summit, next to the column topped with an indignant John Knox, there are superb views of the cathedral below and the city beyond.

(L) The Necropolis, inspired by Père Lachaise cemetery in Paris

Rennie Mackintosh pilgrimage

Architect Charles Rennie Mackintosh (1868–1928) has come to be synonymous with the image of Glasgow, as the creator of buildings of great beauty that idiosyncratically fused Scots Baronial with Gothic, Art Nouveau and modern design. Mackintosh's big break came in 1896, when he won the competition to design a home for the Glasgow School of Art, now sadly damaged by two fires. A number of smaller buildings created during his tenure with the architects Honeyman and Keppie, which began in 1889, document the development of his style. One of his earliest commissions was for a new building to house the *Glasgow Herald*: The Lighthouse, now home to the Mackintosh Interpretation Centre. In the 1890s Glasgow went wild for tearooms, and Mackintosh planned the interiors for what is now the Mackintosh at the Willow. The building that arguably displays the design visionary at his most flamboyant, however, was one he never saw built, the House for an Art Lover, constructed in Bellahouston Park in 1996.

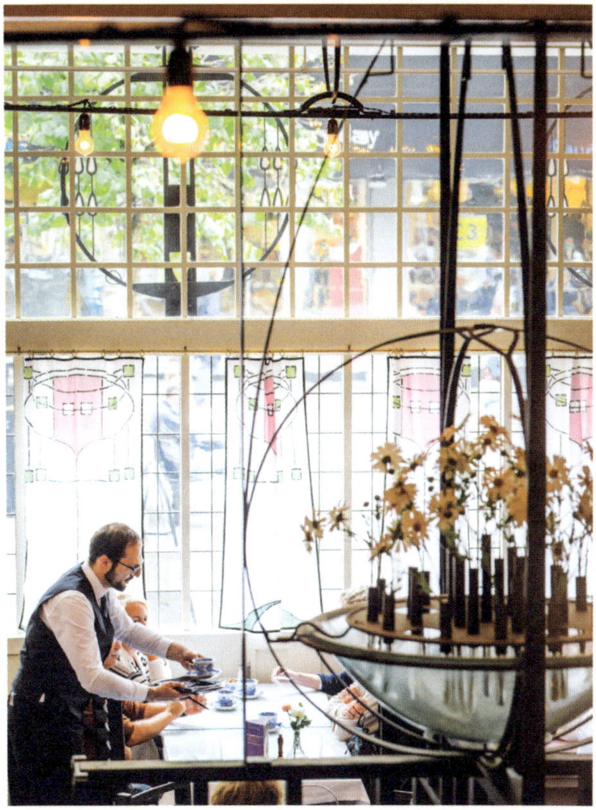

(O) House for an Art Lover; (L) Exhibition at Mackintosh at the Willow; (T, B) One of Glasgow's finest tearooms, Mackintosh at the Willow

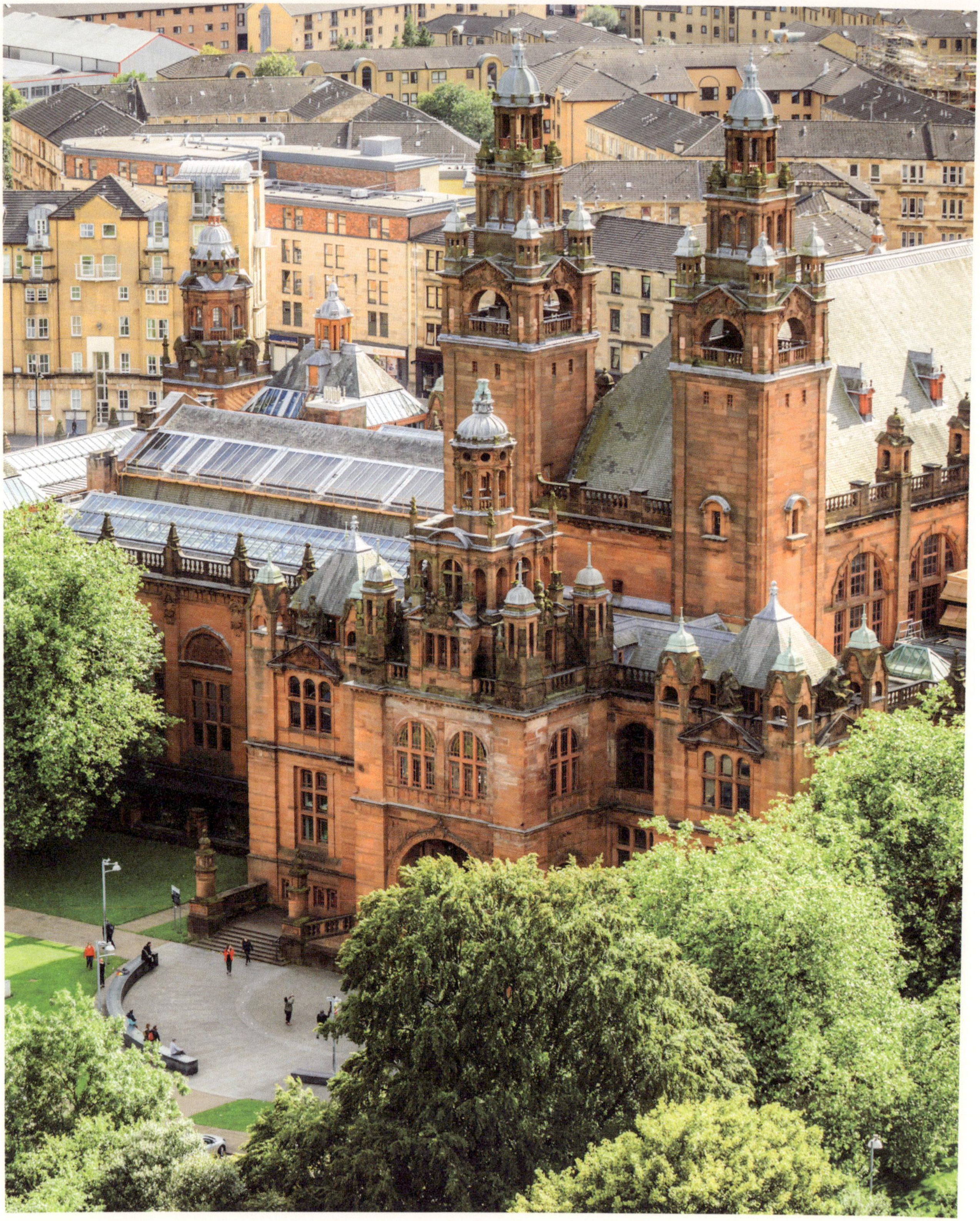

Kelvingrove Art Gallery & Museum

Kelvingrove Art Gallery and Museum is Glasgow's grandest civic showpiece: a Gothic red-sandstone palace of art and artefacts that feels as exuberant and crowd-pleasing as the city itself. Set beside the green sweep of Kelvingrove Park in the West End, it's the kind of museum you can wander without a plan, letting curiosity lead you from room to room. The collection is proudly eclectic, mixing big-name masterpieces with oddities and local treasures, so that a visit becomes a brisk tour through eras, styles and obsessions rather than a dutiful march through "important" things. Among the star turns are works by Dalí, Rembrandt and Van Gogh, but the real joy is the variety: you can drop in for a single gallery and emerge an hour later, pleasantly disoriented, with the sense that Glasgow has quietly shown off again.

(O) The museum's exterior; (L) The East Court; (T) A Van Gogh self-portrait

Argyll & Bute

Cut off for centuries by mountains and sea lochs, Argyll and Bute still feels deliciously remote: a maze of peninsulas and ferry-hop islands where land and water constantly trade places. One moment you're in lush, Gulf-Stream-warmed gardens, the next, on a flat Atlantic outpost with nothing but wind, whisky and wide horizons. In hidden glens lie Celtic and prehistoric relics, while beaches, wildlife and walking routes tempt you further west, towards the ocean's edge.

Fingal's Cave

Five miles southwest of Ulva, Staffa is one of the most dramatic of Scotland's uninhabited islands. On its south side, the sheer rock face features a series of black basalt columns, known as the Colonnade, which have been cut by the sea into cathedral-esque caverns – most notably Fingal's Cave. The Vikings knew the island – the name derives from their word for "Island of Pillars" – Turner sketched it, and it features in Jules Verne's fantasy *The Green Ray*. But Mendelssohn's *Die Fingalshöhle ("Hebrides Overture")*, inspired by the sounds of the sea-wracked caves he heard on a visit here in 1829, did most to popularize the place – after which Queen Victoria gave her blessing, too. The polygonal basalt organ-pipes were created sixty million years ago from a volcanic explosion. The same phenomenon produced the Giant's Causeway in Northern Ireland, and Celtic folk tales often link the two with rival giants Fionn mac Cumhail (Irish) and Fingal (Scottish) throwing rocks at each other across the Irish Sea.

(L) The basalt columns of the island; (T) Staffa: one of the most dramatic of Scotland's uninhabited islands; (B) Fingal's Cave

THE BOATHOUSE

Gigha

Rarely visited and ramshackle, yet all the better for it, this pint-sized speck is one of three outlying islands in the Southern Hebrides that tempt you out into the Atlantic. Like many of the smaller Hebrides, Gigha was bought and sold multiple times after its original lairds, the MacNeils, sold up, and was finally bought by the islanders themselves in 2002. Just six miles by one mile, Gigha has an almost tropical, Gulf Stream location, with tombola beaches, Caribbean-quality palms and the implausibly lovely Boathouse Restaurant serving local halibut and oysters right on the sand. There is just one hotel, one campsite and one ferry, and those who do visit might need to plan ahead, but the rewards are plentiful. Kayak to footprint-free beaches, hike off-road trails with views of Islay, Jura and the distant blur of Ireland, and meander through Achamore Gardens, a 54-acre botanical wonderland. The ferry connects with Kintyre on the mainland.

(O) Boathouse Restaurant on Ardminish Bay; (L) Exotic plants in Achamore Gardens; (T) Only one ferry carts passengers to Gigha

Jura

Twenty-eight miles long and eight wide, the long whale-shaped island of Jura is one of the wildest of the Inner Hebrides, its west coast inaccessible except to the dedicated walker. The distinctive Paps of Jura, so-called because of their breast-like shape, dominate every view off the west coast of Argyll. The island's name is thought to derive from the Norse *dyr-oe* (deer island) and, sure enough, the deer population of 6000 outnumbers the 190 or so humans 33 to 1. With just one road, tracing the east coast, and only one hotel, a few B&Bs and some self-catering cottages, Jura is a tranquil spot with great walking. In April 1946, Eric Blair (AKA George Orwell), moved to the remote north, where he wrote his final novel *1984*. Nearby, the Corryvreckan Whirlpool is thought to be caused by a rocky pinnacle 100ft below the sea, creating standing waves up to 15ft during gale-force winds. The place – *coire bhreacain* (speckled cauldron) in Gaelic – is shrouded in legend concerning *Cailleach* (Hag), the Celtic storm goddess. View it from Carraig Mhor, or take a boat trip from Seil.

(L) The deer population outnumbers the human one by 33 to one on Jura;
(T) The distinctive Paps of Jura; (B) Boat tour to Corryvreckan Whirlpool

Kilmartin

Prehistoric sites are ten-a-penny in Scotland, though few rate as memorably as the one in Kilmartin Glen. Set in mid-Argyll countryside, an extraordinary two-mile-long linear cemetery comprises Neolithic and Bronze Age burial cairns, standing stones and circles, and cup and ring-marked rocks. It likely represents the successive burials of a local wealthy ruling family. Incredibly, there are thought to be 350 ancient monuments within a six-mile radius of Kilmartin. For the best views, scramble to the top of Dunadd Fort, on Mòine Mhór – the Great Moss, now a nature reserve. A modest but historically significant mound, Dunadd was once the seat of the Gaelic kings, Dal Riata. For an overview of the region's outstanding cultural landscape, visit the excellent Kilmartin Museum.

(O) View from Dunadd Fort; (L) Temple Wood stone circle; (T) The standing stones of Kilmartin Glen; (B) Achnabreac prehistoric rock art

Mount Stuart

(T) The huge Italianate Gothic mansion is adorned with lavish decoration

The lovely Isle of Bute, accessed by ferry from Wemyss Bay, is generally a modest beach-holiday destination, within a pebble's throw of Glasgow. But all sense of modesty was chucked into the Firth of Clyde when the Marquess of Bute, an architect and eccentric, created Mount Stuart. The original family home was almost destroyed by fire in 1877 and the new abode, containing the surviving contents of the old, is a huge Italianate Gothic mansion adorned with lavish decoration. A railway line had to be specially created to haul the tons of shimmering white Carrara marble used for the construction of the Marble Chapel. Elsewhere, stained-glass windows depict the signs of the zodiac – the marquess had a penchant for mysticism – as well as images from the natural world: look out for a carved frog playing a lute, squirrels foraging in the dining room panelling and painted monkeys reading in the library.

Tiree

The most westerly of the Inner Hebridean isles, treeless Tiree rewards those who make the considerable effort to get here with distinctive architecture, incredible flora and fauna, and shimmering beaches. It also boasts more sunshine than any other place in Scotland – well, that's what the locals will tell you. Above all, though, the island is synonymous with surf. While Scotland has no shortage of amazing places to hit the waves, ask any surfer – wave, wind or kite – and they will tell you that Tiree is tops. The best months to surf are those either side of July and August, when the powerful offshore winds offer optimum conditions. The season climaxes in October when the world's finest surfers descend on the sands for the Tiree Wave Classic, the longest-running pro-surf competition in the calendar. It's an absolute blast, with much partying taking place alongside the serious business of the sport itself.

(L) Triagh Thodrasdail beach; (T) Tiree is peppered with traditional crofts; (B) Tiree Wave Classic

Tobermory

Mull's chief town, Tobermory, at the northern tip of the island, is easily the most attractive fishing port on the west coast of Scotland, its clusters of brightly coloured houses and boats sheltering in a bay backed by a steep bluff. Founded in 1788, it never really took off as a fishing port and only survived due to the steady influx of crofters evicted from other parts of the island during the Clearances. It is now the most important, and by far the most vibrant, settlement on Mull, and if you've got young kids, you'll instantly recognize it as the place where *Balamory* was filmed. The harbour – known as Main Street – is one long parade of candy-coloured hotels, guesthouses, restaurants and shops. The rest of the upper town offers great views over the bay. Be sure to call by the Mull Aquarium, Europe's first catch-and-release aquarium, meaning all marine life is released within four weeks, then pause for a dram in the Tobermory Distillery.

(O) Tobermory's multicoloured harbour;
(L) Tours and tastings are available at Tobermory Distillery;
(T) The upper town offers great bay views

Treshnish Isles

Northwest of Staffa lie the Treshnish Isles, an archipelago of uninhabited volcanic islets, none more than a mile or two across. The most distinctive is Bac Mór, shaped like a Puritan's hat and popularly dubbed the Dutchman's Cap. Lunga, the largest island, is a summer nesting place for hundreds of seabirds, in particular guillemots, razorbills and puffins; the last of these are far and away the star attraction, and, for many, the main reason for visiting. It's also a major breeding ground for seals. From April to October several operators offer boat trips to the Treshnish Isles. The two most northerly islands, Cairn na Burgh More and Cairn na Burgh Beg, have remains of ruined castles, the first of which served as a lookout post for the Lords of the Isles and was last garrisoned in the Civil War; Cairn na Burgh Beg hasn't been occupied since the 1715 Jacobite uprising.

(L) Lunga is a major breeding ground for seals; (T) Atlantic puffins steal the show on Lunga; (B) Sunrise over the Treshnish Isles

THE BOATHOUSE

Ulva

Located off the southwest of Mull, Ulva is a magical, time-stopped place that's almost lost in the fold of the map. For decades, this island of no cars, no shops, no postcards and no cheery tour guides, was home to only six residents, a shoreline café and two bothies (shelters), both 7km from the boat jetty. But rather than face further depopulation like so many Scottish islands, the locals took matters into their own hands, shaping a community buyout in 2018. Now, the Storas Ulbha cultural heritage centre is in the pipeline, alongside new accommodation, and this island time-capsule is in the throes of a renaissance. The rewards for visitors are sightings of Scotland's big five (golden eagles, red deer, otters, seals, harbour porpoise), closeness to nature, and peace. The Ulva Ferry runs in summer by demand only.

(L) The Boathouse, Ulva's only café

Iona

Tiny Iona has an outsized presence in Scotland's imagination – a sliver of land off Mull where faith and legend tangle in the sea air. The island's pull begins at the shore, where the Atlantic light turns everything crisp, then deepens as you walk inland towards the Abbey. This is pilgrimage territory, not just in the religious sense, but as a journey into the roots of Scotland's story. Columba fled here from Ireland in 563 and founded a monastery that helped spark the conversion of the pagan Scots; later, after Viking attacks, Benedictine monks restored and rebuilt parts of the site around 1200. Follow the island's own pilgrimage trail from rocky St Ronan's Bay past the ruins of an Augustinian nunnery, pausing at St Martin's Cross with its later carvings. The Abbey and its crosses give the place a solemn centre, yet Iona never feels purely museum-like: it's too open to wind, weather and changing skies. Outside, the island keeps things simple – beaches, machair, and quiet lanes where the loudest sound can be your own footsteps.

(O) Iona has been a focus of pilgrimage since Columba fled here in 563; (L) St Martin's Cross; (T) Sunset at Iona; (B) Iona Abbey cloisters

Stirling, Loch Lomond & the Trossachs

Once the only gateway from Scotland's fertile heartlands to the rugged north, this region still feels like a threshold: crag-top castles, old battle ground, and roads that quickly trade city streets for lochs and forests. Stirling's history hangs in the air, while westward the scenery turns romantic and wild – islands, mountain paths and long waterside views in the Trossachs and around Loch Lomond. It's a place for big stories by day, and quiet, starry lochside nights.

Argaty Red Kites

Twitchers, kids, wildlife fans... pretty much anyone will find a visit to Argaty Red Kites irresistible. Located just outside the handsome village of Doune, the working farm provides a feeding station for the once-persecuted red kites, whose russet-hued feathers, forked tails, serene floating motion and huge wingspan make them gratifyingly easy to identify. Argaty was involved in the reintroduction of red kites, which were hunted to near-extinction in the UK in the 1950s, and numbers have since recovered. Tucked in a hide, you can watch the birds' acrobatics as they swoop down to feed, while rangers give you lively background on the majestic creatures. You can also spot red squirrels, buzzards, peregrine falcons and kestrels. Not just an advocate for feathered friends, Argaty Red Kites also assisted in the relocation of a family of beavers to the farm in 2021. These wonderful creatures, known as nature's engineers, help reduce flooding and increase biodiversity. A second family joined them in early 2022, and these impressive rewilding achievements have put the centre on the conservation map.

(L) Kites diving for food; (T) Red Kite Viewing Hide; (B) Red Kite with carrion in its beak

Inchcailloch

(T) Inchcailloch is carpeted in bluebells in spring

On the eastern shore of Loch Lomond, the tiny waterside settlement of Balmaha straddles the Highland Boundary Fault. If you stand on the viewpoint above the pier, you can see the fault line clearly marked by the series of woody islands that form giant stepping stones across the loch. The closest to the shore, Inchcailloch was extensively planted with oaks to provide bark for the local tanning industry. Now owned by the Scottish Natural Heritage, the forested speck is encircled by a two-mile nature trail, which passes the ruins of a fourteenth-century nunnery and associated burial ground, a picnic and camping site, and a sandy beach. Until the mid-seventeenth century parishioners on the far (western) shore of Loch Lomond used to row across to Inchcailloch for Sunday services at the church linked to the nunnery. Today, a small ferry carts visitors across the water, with departures on demand.

Lake of Menteith

Scotland has few more romantic spots than the Lake of Menteith. The only lake in the country – the rest of them are termed 'lochs' – sits just to the east of the mighty Trossachs. The hill and mountain views in all directions are sublime, as are the clear waters encircled by woodland. A good access point is the Karma Lake of Menteith hotel, which is also an excellent food stop. From here you can wander to the shore for a dip at one of the secluded stony beaches or, better still, catch the little ferry that nips across the lake to its uninhabited island, Inchmahome. Once on this tiny emerald speck, wander through the ancient woodland to the thirteenth-century ruins of an Augustinian abbey, still graceful despite its decline. Mary, Queen of Scots played here as a five-year-old – she was hidden on the island before being taken to France. Indeed, local legend says that the chestnut trees, with their leaning, twisted trunks, were planted by her.

(O) Port of Menteith Church; (L) A motorboat ferry whisks visitors to Inchmahome Priory; (T) Fishing on the lake at sunset

Loch Lomond

The largest stretch of fresh water in Britain – 23 miles long and up to five wide – Loch Lomond is the epitome of Scottish scenic splendour, thanks in large part to the ballad that fondly recalls its "bonnie, bonnie banks". The Loch Lomond and the Trossachs National Park covers over seven hundred square miles of scenic territory from Loch Long in Cowal to Loch Earn and Loch Tay, on the south-west fringes of Perthshire. The centrepiece is undoubtedly Loch Lomond, and the most popular gateway is Balloch at the loch's southern tip. Very different in tone, the verdant eastern side of the loch, abutting the Trossachs, operates at a slower pace, with wooden ferryboats puttering out to tree-covered islands off the village of Balmaha. If you're looking for a relatively easy climb with an impressive view over Loch Lomond, start at Balmaha for the ascent of Conic Hill (1175ft), a two- to three-hour round-trip walk through forest and open hillside.

(L) The Maid of the Loch paddle steamer at Balloch Pier; (T) View from Conic Hill;
(B) Explore Loch Lomond by pedal boat, canoe or bike

Stirling Castle

Taking a winding walk up the lanes of the Old Town of Stirling is the best way to approach its wonderful castle, which sits proud and defensive on a high crag looking west towards the Trossach Mountains. The sheer 250ft castle crag was first fortified in the Iron Age, but the building you see today dates from the fifteenth and sixteenth centuries, the golden age of the city of Stirling, when it was the favourite residence of the Stuart monarchy. Highlights of the building, aside from sweeping battlement views, include its mighty Great Hall with a hammer-beam roof hewn from 35 oaks; the Stirling Heads, oak medallions carved with portraits of royal, Biblical and mythological figures; the tranquil Queen Anne Gardens; and the impressive palace tapestries, born out of a fourteen-year research and weaving project.

(O, L) Stirling Castle sitting proud on Castle Hill, a rocky precipice; (T) Sculpture on the Prince's Walk; (B) View of Stirling from the top of the National Wallace Monument

THE Kelpies

You don't expect mythic beasts on the edge of the Central Belt, but that's exactly what you find in Helix Park in Falkirk. Rising from parkland like something half-surfaced from a dark loch, the Kelpies are colossal horse heads that nod to Scotland's folklore of shape-shifting water spirits, while also tipping the hat to the working horses that once hauled industry along canals. Up close, the engineering is part of the spectacle – metal plates, muscular curves, and faces that shift expression with the light. It's a rare modern landmark that feels properly Scottish rather than imported, and the heads are undoubtedly bold, slightly eerie, and impossible to ignore. Time your visit for dusk, when lighting turns the whole scene cinematic, with the silhouettes cutting into a bruised sky. For visual impact and sheer oddball confidence, few places compete.

(L) The Kelpies from above, and Helix Park; (T) Pathway around the park; (B) The sculptures at dawn

Welcome to
Scottish Canals
The Falkirk Wheel

THE Falkirk Wheel

If Scotland had to choose a single piece of modern engineering to show off, the Falkirk Wheel would be a strong candidate. Part sculpture, part machine, it lifts boats between canals with an elegance that makes the mechanics feel almost incidental. Watching it work is oddly hypnotic: slow rotation, water held steady, and then the quiet satisfaction of a vessel gliding out at a different level as if that's perfectly normal. Even aside from the impressiveness of the Wheel, the setting is worth lingering in, with the proliferation of surrounding waterways, towpaths and viewpoints, ideal whether you're cycling, walking, or hopping on a boat trip to see the Wheel in action. In a country famous for castles and glens, this is a reminder that Scottish ingenuity can be just as memorable as its landscapes.

(L) The Wheel

Fife

Barely fifty miles across, Fife is small but proudly distinct – the ancient Kingdom set between the Tay, the Forth and the cold North Sea. It's a place of quick-changing moods: gentle inland hills and old villages give way to windswept cliffs, rocky bays and sandy beaches, with sea light sharpening every view. Harbours and cobbled lanes feel timeless, while the coastline invites long, bracing walks and seafood stops. Come for history, stay for the salt-air calm.

Crail Harbour

Crail is the archetypally photogenic East Neuk fishing village, its maze of rough cobbled streets leading steeply down to a tiny stone-built harbour surrounded by piles of lobster creels. Fishermen's cottages are tucked into every nook and cranny in the cliff. Beyond the harbour is a sand beach, and above are perched the grander merchants' houses, as well as the twelfth-century church where John Knox once delivered a damning sermon rallying against the local fishermen for working on Sundays. The village still has a working harbour, and if the boats have been out you can often buy fresh lobster and crab cooked to order on the water's edge. Reilly Shellfish, a little wooden shack down at the harbour, cooks the freshest takeaway lobster you're ever likely to find. Take your pick from the condemned crustaceans scuttling around the tank next to the shack.

(O) Fishing boats bob in the harbour; (L) Crail's cobbled streets; (T) The village is rooted in fishing heritage; (B) Lobster creels

Culross

The beautifully preserved seventeenth-century village of Culross on the Fife coast is a gem of a place, with cobbled streets, gabled houses and even its own palace and abbey. The presence of such grand buildings in such of an out-of-the-way spot is due to the village's early invention of undersea coal extraction. Wealthy merchant George Bruce built Culross Palace in the late 1700s: it's a rambling ochre-painted place with wood panelling, decorated ceilings and a garden planted with herbs and vegetables of the period. Up the hill, past rows of cottages with crow-stepped gables and plenty of intriguing passageways to lead you off course, you'll find the remnants of Culross Abbey. Founded by Cistercian monks on land given to the Church in 1217 by the earl of Fife, the nave of the original building is a ruin. The choir of the abbey became the parish church in 1633; a tenth-century Celtic cross in the north transept nods to the abbey's origins. Outside, the eighteenth-century gravestones are strikingly carved with symbols of the deceased person's occupation.

(L) Culross Palace; (T) The beautifully preserved seventeenth-century cottages of Culross; (B) Inside the Palace

Dunfermline Abbey & Palace

Dunfermline Abbey is a stone monolith from the Middle Ages. Queen Margaret began building a Benedictine priory in 1072 (still visible beneath the nave of the present church), and her son, David I, raised the priory to the rank of abbey the following century. In 1303, during the Wars of Independence, most of the monastic buildings were destroyed by the English King Edward I's troops. Robert the Bruce helped rebuild the abbey and when he died was buried here minus his heart, which was sent, unsuccessfully, on a pilgrimage to the Holy Land, only to be buried at Melrose Abbey. Inside, the stained glass is impressive, and the thick columns are carved with chevrons, spirals and arrowheads. The guesthouse of Queen Margaret's Benedictine monastery became the palace in the sixteenth century under James VI, who gave both it and the abbey to his consort, Queen Anne of Denmark. Charles I, the last monarch to be born in Scotland, entered the world here in 1600. Today, all that is left of the palace is a long sandstone facade: a striking silhouette against the sky at dusk.

(L) Thick columns carved with chevrons, spirals and arrowheads

Falkland Palace

A hunting retreat to the Stewart kings for two hundred years, the construction of Falkland Palace began at the behest of James IV in 1500, and was completed by James V. Charles II stayed here in 1650 when he was in Scotland for his coronation, but after the Jacobite rising of 1715 and temporary occupation by Rob Roy the palace was abandoned, remaining so until the late nineteenth century when it was acquired by the third marquess of Bute. He restored the palace, and today it is a stunning example of early Renaissance architecture, with corbelled parapet, mullioned windows, round towers and massive walls. Inside there's a stately drawing room, a Chapel Royal (still used for Mass) and a Tapestry Gallery with seventeenth-century Flemish hangings. Outside, herbaceous borders line a pristine lawn. Look out for the high walls of the oldest real (or royal) tennis court in Britain – built in 1539 for James V and still in use.

(L) Stained-glass windows in the Chapel Royal and Tapestry Gallery; (T) The Renaissance palace is surrounded by extensive gardens; (B) Britain's oldest real tennis court is still in action

St Andrews' beaches

(T) East Sands, part of the Fife Coastal Path

Though better known for its prestigious, ancient university (est. 1410) and world-class golf status, St Andrews also boasts two gorgeous sandy beaches. At the northern edge of the town is West Sands, immortalized in 1981 historical sports drama film *Chariots of Fire* as the spot where the Olympians run in slow motion, across the sand and through the surf, to a soundtrack by by Vangelis. Stretching for two miles and backed by dunes and fairways, it's still much loved by runners, strollers, sandcastle-makers and birdwatchers: you may spot skylarks, meadow pipits and sand buntings here, and possibly the rarer ringed plover. The more compact East Sands sits by the city's harbour. Part of the Fife Coastal Path, this similarly lovely golden swathe is popular not only with walkers but also surfers and sailing enthusiasts.

St Andrews Links – THE Old Course

Even if you couldn't care less about golf, the Old Course still earns its place through sheer atmosphere. The landscape has been shaped by wind, sand and tradition, and in this spot, the game's rituals have been repeated so often they've become part of the place itself. The Old Course's sense of continuity is essential to its significance, from the "hallowed" eighteenth fairway and the Swilken Bridge, to the sightlines that have framed generations of drama and triumph. But the real significance runs deeper than the photo spots. This is where the modern game was codified and measured, and it's the original template against which every other course is quietly compared. It doesn't feel like a manicured show-piece so much as a living commons for golf: demanding and exposed. And everywhere you look there are reminders of the long roll-call of champions who've walked these same humps and hollows.

(L) Swilcan Bridge casting a shadow on the lush green of the Old Course

Isle of May

The Isle of May is close enough to Fife to feel like a day-trip, yet once you land it has the brisk, salt-stung clarity of a proper outpost. The island's main draw is wildlife – a compact stage where seabirds, seals and sea-spray do most of the talking – and in season the place hums with life. Paths lead past low cliffs and grassy slopes to viewpoints where the sea feels big and busy, with boats and weather rolling through. It's the kind of place that rewards binoculars and patience, but it's also satisfying at a simpler level, thanks to its clean air, wide horizons, and the sense of being temporarily removed from mainland routines. Photographers love it for good reason, too – birds on the wing, rock textures, and light that changes mood faster than you can swap lenses.

(L) Guillemots nesting on the cliffs; (T) Sea cliffs; (B) A birdwatcher observes seabirds near the lighthouse

Perthshire

Genteel, attractive Perthshire is, in many ways, the epitome of well-groomed rural Scotland: gentle glens, mature woodland, rushing rivers and peaceful lochs – long favoured by a well-to-do country set. Ancient Perth sits at the mouth of the Tay, a historic gateway towards the Highlands, while beyond lie neat towns and villages amid fertile straths. Head north and west and the landscape gathers into bigger mountains, quieter roads and wild, empty spaces.

Blair Castle

(T) Blair Castle: the seat of the Atholl dukedom

Seat of the Atholl dukedom, whitewashed, turreted Blair Castle, surrounded by parkland and dating from 1269, presents an impressive sight as you approach it up the drive. You might even spot a piper, one of the Atholl Highlanders, playing in front of the castle; this select group was retained by the duke as his own infantry – a unique privilege afforded to him by Queen Victoria, who stayed here in 1844. Visit in May for the Atholl Highlanders Parade, the annual parade and inspection of Britain's last private army by their colonel-in-chief, the Duke of Atholl, on the eve of their Highland Games. Thirty or so rooms display a selection of paintings, antique furniture and plasterwork that is sumptuous in the extreme. Highlights are the soaring entrance hall, with every spare inch of wood panelling covered in weapons of some description, and the vast ballroom, with its timber roof, antlers and mixture of portraits.

Drummond Castle Gardens

Of all the attractions around Crieff, most impressive are the magnificent Drummond Castle Gardens. The approach, up a splendid avenue of beech trees, is pretty enough, but by crossing the courtyard of the castle to the grand terrace you can view the garden in all its symmetrical glory. It was begun as early as 1630 (the date of the tall central sundial), though the design of the French/Italianate parterre is Victorian: it depicts a St Andrew's cross and incorporates other images associated with the Drummonds, including two crowns and the wavy motif found on the family crest. Italian marble statues punctuate the long lines of the cross, and the overall effect is of exceptional harmony and grace. Beyond the terraced gardens unfurls spacious parkland; a peaceful spot to walk. The castle itself is closed to visitors.

(O) Drummond Castle Gardens is the finest attraction around Crieff; (L) The garden in all its symmetrical glory; (T) The terraced gardens are a peaceful haven; (B) The castle itself is closed, but the garden alone warrants a visit

Gleneagles Hotel

Iconic Gleneagles is famously home to three championship golf courses and enclosed in 850 acres of Perthshire countryside, an hour's drive from Edinburgh. The five-star hotel has welcomed leaders and celebrities from every corner of the globe, but the status is justified. There's a plush spa and health club with two pools, sauna, steam room, hot tub, gym, indoor and outdoor tennis courts and a jam-packed programme of country pursuits, from horse riding to gundog training and falconry. If staying the night at the hotel is beyond your means, consider eating at the refreshingly unstuffy Andrew Fairlie at Gleneagles (offering a three-course à la carte menu). It has two Michelin stars and is perhaps the finest restaurant in all of Scotland, serving up dynamic dishes like roast turbot with spiced verjus sauce.

(L) An artful mix of classic and contemporary interiors; (T) The five-star hotel is set in extensive grounds; (B) The eighteenth hole on the PGA Centenary course

PERTHSHIRE

Glenturret

Dating back to 1775, Glenturret claims to be the oldest working whisky distillery in Scotland. Today it is still one of the more attractive, with low-slung whitewashed buildings set in woodland beside the gurgling River Turret. Even if whisky isn't your priority, the on-site dining might entice a visit. In 2021, a fine-dining restaurant was opened in a converted pagoda, in part thanks to Lalique, the French glassmaker and Glenturret stakeholder; it has since been awarded two Michelin stars. Glasgow-born chef Mark Donald, of Number One at The Balmoral in Edinburgh, is the man behind the menu – inventive dishes may include locally sourced spring lamb, foraged white asparagus and morels, and haggis waffle. Whisky makes its way on to the dinner table (and not just in tumblers), weaved subtly into the likes of sourdough made with malted barley from the adjacent mill.

(L) Fine whisky; (T) Glenturret claims to be the oldest working whisky distillery in Scotland; (B) The elegant restaurant

Rannoch Moor

Rannoch Moor occupies roughly 150 square miles of uninhabited and uninhabitable peat bogs, lochs, heather hillocks, strewn lumps of granite and gnarled Caledonian pines, all 1000ft above sea level. Perhaps the most striking thing about the moor is its inaccessibility: one road, between Crianlarich and Glen Coe, skirts its western side, while another struggles west from Pitlochry to reach its eastern edge. The only regular transport here is the West Highland Railway, which stops at Rannoch and, a little to the north, Corrour, which has no road access at all – though it does have a great café. Corrour stole an unlikely scene in the film *Trainspotting* when the four central characters headed here for a taste of the great outdoors; a wooden SYHA hostel is located a mile away on the shores of Loch Ossian and can only be reached on foot. From Rannoch station, beside which is the isolated Moor of Rannoch Restaurant & Rooms, it's possible to catch the train to Corrour and walk the nine miles back; it's a longer slog to Glen Coe, the dramatic peaks of which poke up above the moor's western horizon. Determined hillwalkers will find a clutch of Munros around Corrour, including remote Ben Alder, 3765ft high above the forbidding shores of Loch Ericht.

(L) Rannoch Viaduct

SEAWELL
ABERDEEN

Northeast Scotland

The northeast of Scotland is a big, sea-facing sweep of the country: a triangle of land thrusting into the North Sea, where undulating farmland gives way to wooded glens, mountains and an increasingly rugged coastline of high cliffs and long sandy beaches with the widest skies and room to roam. Granite-built cities and small ports bring a bracing, salt-air energy, while inland you'll find quiet valleys, rivers and a scattering of ancient stones and dramatic castles.

Aberdeen

The third-largest city in Scotland, Aberdeen lies 120 miles northeast of Edinburgh on the banks of the rivers Dee and Don. Since the 1970s, oil has made Aberdeen a wealthy place, but the Granite City is more than a departure point for the transient 15,000-strong population who live on the 130 oil platforms out at sea. Its architecture is stunning – a granite cityscape created in the nineteenth century. Classical inspiration and Gothic Revival styles predominate, giving grace to a material once thought of as only good enough for tombs and paving stones. The city centre features the opulent Marischal College, the colonnaded Aberdeen Art Gallery and the burgeoning nightlife of Belmont Street. Union Street leads west to the gentrified shopping centres and raucous bars that define the West End. To the south, the harbour still heaves with fishing boats, while north of the centre lies attractive Old Aberdeen, a village neighbourhood presided over by King's College, St Machar's Cathedral and a stunning modern university library. In addition, the urban parks are some of the most beautiful in Britain.

(L) Union Terrace Gardens; (T) Marischal College; (B) P&J Live, a modern events space

Arbroath smokehouses

Local fishermen have been landing their catches at Arbroath since it was settled in the twelfth century. About fifteen miles northeast of Dundee, the harbour town is situated on the Angus coast where it starts to curve in from the North Sea towards the Firth of Tay. The name of the town stems from Aber Brothock, the burn which runs into the sea here, and it certainly has a great location, with long sandy beaches and stunning sandstone cliffs on either side of town, as well as an attractive old working harbour. The town's most famous product is the Arbroath smokie – line-caught haddock, smoke-cured over smouldering oak chips. The local delicacy is still made here in a number of family-run smokehouses tucked in around the harbour. Some of the best places to try the dish include But'n'Ben, M & M Spink – whose smoke-warmed fish Rick Stein described as "a world-class delicacy", and The Old Brewhouse.

(O) The Arbroath smokie: line-caught haddock, smoke-cured over smouldering oak chips; (L) Lobster creels piled by Arbroath Harbour; (R) Rick Stein is a big fan of M & M Spink

Dunnottar Castle

(T) The Castle

One of Scotland's finest ruined castles, Dunnottar Castle is a huge ninth-century fortress set on a three-sided sheer cliff jutting into the sea – a location striking enough to be chosen as the backdrop for Zeffirelli's film version of *Hamlet*. Once the principal fortress of the northeast, the mainly fifteenth- and sixteenth-century ruins are worth a good root around, and there are many dramatic views out to the crashing sea. Siege and bloodstained drama splatter the castle's past: in 1297 the whole English Plantagenet garrison was burnt alive here by William Wallace, while one of the more gruesome tales from the castle's history tells of the imprisonment and torture of 122 men and 45 women Covenanters in 1685 – an event, as it says on the Covenanters' Stone in the churchyard, "whose dark shadow is for evermore flung athwart the Castled Rock".

Fife Arms

The Fife Arms is no shy and retiring wallflower. The interiors are a playful blend of wild romanticism and sumptuous maximalism; think contemporary art, one-off antiques, oriental rugs, richly textured fabrics. It's hardly surprising when you consider the design duo behind the interiors: creative power couple Iwan and Manuela Wirth, of the Hauser & Wirth art galleries. Look out for Chinese artist Zhang Engli's extraordinary painted ceiling, a pencil sketch of a stag drawn in 1874 by Queen Victoria, and the handblown neon glass deer chandelier by Los Angeles-based artist Richard Jackson. If you can tear your eyes away from the design drama, windows frame tantalizing glimpses of mountains. There's a spa for bespoke face and body treatments, a drawing room for afternoon tea, and a fabulous whisky bar for knocking back a dram (365 varieties line the walls). Blow away the cobwebs the next day with a bracing hike through the Cairngorms National Park.

(L) The hotel in winter; (T) Design power couple Iwan and Manuela Wirth, of the Hauser & Wirth art galleries, are behind the interiors; (B) Decor is a playful mix of wild romanticism and sumptuous maximalism

V&A Dundee

In the nineteenth century Dundee was Britain's main processor of jute, which earned the city the tag "Juteopolis". The decline of manufacturing wasn't kind to the 145,000-strong population, who are still living with its effects. However, regeneration is today's big buzzword, with some drawing comparisons with Glasgow's reinvention in the 1980s and 1990s. A major star of the cultural scene is the V&A Dundee, a waterfront design museum in a ship-like modern building, designed by Japanese architect Kengo Kuma as a homage to the city's shipping heritage and rugged rock-strewn coastline. The two upended stone-clad pyramid are unflinchingly modern, and provide an interesting foil to the lofty masts of the neighbouring *Discovery* vessel. The main attraction is the (free) Scottish Design Galleries, whose highlight is a brilliant reconstruction of Charles Rennie Mackintosh's Ingram Street Tearooms. Other exhibits celebrate the country's painters, fashionistas and illustrators, including the creator of Dundee's own cartoon hero Dennis the Menace. Look out for an ornate panel fragment from the Titanic, a winged Cartier headdress studded with diamonds, and Natalie Portman's *Star Wars* costume.

(L) The striking exterior

THE Great Glen & River Spey

The Great Glen is a vast geological fault line – a huge rift valley carved and polished by glaciers – that slices diagonally across the Highlands from Fort William to Inverness, funnelling you between lochs and mountains. At one end, Ben Nevis and sea lochs deliver rugged drama; at the other, Inverness opens the door to the north. Nearby, the River Spey runs through whisky-soaked Speyside, where forests, salmon rivers and big Cairngorm views entice you onward.

Cairngorms National Park

The Cairngorms are Scotland on a bigger scale than you expect: a national park covering almost 1,750 square miles – the biggest in Britain – and anchored by the Cairngorms massif, the UK's largest mountainscape and the only sizeable plateau in the country above 2,500ft. The name itself hints at the mood, from the Gaelic *An Carm Gorm* – "the blue hill" – after the bluish-tinged stones found here. The park isn't just about height, either: it holds a quarter of Scotland's native woodland and a quarter of the UK's threatened wildlife species, with the ancient Caledonian forest at Rothiemurchus even home to red squirrels. Aviemore is the classic gateway for outdoor pursuits, though you can also come in from Perthshire, Deeside or Donside. And the sense of distance is real: the only road connection across the range, the A939 from Tomintoul to Cock Bridge, is often impassable in winter snow, while on foot the old cattle-drovers' route of the Lairig Ghru makes for a very long day's walk.

(O) Loch an Eilein in Rothiemurchus Forest; (L) Reindeer in the Cairngorms National Park; (T) Cairngorm Ski Resort; (B) The ancient Caledonian forest at Rothiemurchus

Glen Coe

Breathtakingly beautiful Glen Coe ("Valley of Weeping"), sixteen miles south of Fort William, is a spectacular mountain valley between forbidding peaks, their conical tops often wreathed in cloud. Not just a place of dramatic beauty, Glen Coe is also rooted in high historical drama. In 1692 this was the site of a terrible government massacre, aimed to supress the supposedly lawless MacDonald clan. Campbell of Glenlyon was ordered to billet his soldiers with the MacDonalds of Glen Coe, and the soldiers received ten days of warm Highland hospitality from the clan. Then the soldiers turned on their hosts, killing more than forty people and causing over three hundred to flee into a February blizzard. The National Trust's eco-friendly visitor centre in the glen outlines this troubling story and its repercussions, as well as giving guidance on outstanding walks in the area. There are also interesting exhibits on ecology and conservation issues. Glencoe village is a handy base, where the heather-roofed Glencoe Folk Museum brings eighteenth-century crofting to vivid life.

(L) The River Coupall and Stob Dearg (Buachaille Etive Mor)

Loch Ness

Loch Ness is one of the most important stomping grounds in the Scottish Highlands. Though it is best known for the long-necked cryptid lurking in its depths, there is so much more to the loch than Nessie-chasing tours. For starters, it's a hiker's paradise, where pine-skirted mountains plunge into mirror-clear waters. Scramble up Meall Fuar-mhonaidh, Loch Ness' highest hill at 699m, or tackle the corkscrew route between Foyers and Dores on the lesser-trodden eastern shore. Test your mettle on the Great Glen Way or South Loch Ness Trail; together, they form the Loch Ness 360° Trail, a 106km-long circuit that takes three to six days to hike or bike. Beyond the toothy ramparts of Urquhart Castle, Fort Augustus is the start of the nineteenth-century Caledonian Canal, a 96km hand-dug waterway that leads budding houseboat captains south to Corpach near Fort William.

(L) Urquhart Castle; (T) Nessie-chasing tours are popular on Loch Ness; (B) Suidhe Viewpoint offers excellent loch views

Speyside Whisky Trail

There are more distilleries concentrated in the Speyside "whisky triangle" – a small area stretching from Craigellachie, down towards Tomintoul in the south and east to Huntly – than in any other part of Scotland. The region's hub, Dufftown, boasts no fewer than nine distilleries and is a popular base for a tour of whisky country. Fewer visitors venture to the more remote glens, such as Glenlivet, nestled into which is Britain's highest village, Tomintoul. The 65 mile-long Speyside Way, with its beguiling blend of mountains, river, wildlife and whisky, is fast establishing itself as a popular long-distance footpath. Starting at Buckie on the Moray Firth coast, it follows the River Spey from Spey Bay south to Aviemore, with branches linking it to Dufftown and Tomintoul. The route is a five- to seven-day expedition, but for shorter walks or cycling trips head to the stretch between Craigellachie and Glenlivet; several distilleries all lie directly on or close to the route.

(O) Glenlivet distillery; (L) Speyside Way; (T) Whisky tasting

Ben Nevis

(T) The North face of Ben Nevis looking towards Fort William and Loch Eli

Ben Nevis is a blunt fact of geography – Britain's highest mountain – but it's also a rite of passage, a weather-maker, and the looming backdrop that gives Fort William its edge. The classic ascent is achievable for fit walkers, which is part of the mountain's appeal: it's a big day out rather than an alpine expedition, yet it still demands respect. Conditions can switch quickly, with cloud swallowing the summit and wind turning a straightforward climb into something more serious. On a clear day, the views are the payoff – ridgelines and lochs against that immense Highland spread that makes you feel happily small. Ben Nevis isn't special just because it's the highest hill around, but because it packs Scotland's mountain mood into one blunt, uncompromising lump of rock – busy on the lower paths, yet still properly wild once you're up on the plateau.

Glenfinnan Viaduct

The Glenfinnan Viaduct is the sort of Victorian engineering that manages to be both muscular and elegant. A 21-arch sweep of stone, it traces a lovely arc across an improbably emerald glen, looking as if it has always belonged there. The drama peaks when the Jacobite steam train (the famous Fort William–Mallaig service) comes chuffing over the top in a cloud of steam – a scene that was popular long before the *Harry Potter* hype, even if the "Hogwarts Express" nickname now keeps seats in high demand. But you don't need perfect timing to enjoy it. Stand back and the whole structure reads as a clean, confident line in the landscape; get closer and you feel the heft of the masonry, the repetition of arches and the serious intent behind the romance. The setting does the rest of the work – moorland textures, water and distant peaks shifting with the weather, so the same view can look soft one minute and stark the next.

(L, T, B) The dramatic form of the viaduct

The North & Northwest Highlands

Single-track roads, Gaelic radio and weather that changes fast: the north and northwest Highlands feels like nowhere else in Britain. Bare mountains, remote glens and dark lochs tumble towards a magnificent coastline of cliffs, white-sand bays and sea stacks. The peat bogs in the far north are among Europe's most unspoilt wildernesses, and some crofting villages are still reachable only by boat. Here, you feel yourself on the very edge of the world.

Ardnamurchan

The most westerly point on the British mainland, Ardnamurchan is as remote as it is inspiring, with its endless sea vistas and empty beaches. The gateway to the region is the former lead-mining village of Strontian, from where a mostly single-track road weaves its way all along the southern shore, which itself bounds the northern rim of Loch Sunart, the longest sea loch in the country. It is unquestionably one of the loveliest drives in all of Scotland. But it's not one you can, or should, rush; not only does this drive necessitate patience, but there are diversions aplenty, such as the engaging Ardnamurchan Natural History Visitor Centre. The best bit, however, is Ardnamurchan Point, crowned by a splendid lighthouse designed by Alan Stevenson (uncle of Robert Louis) and, a few miles north of here, the magnificent belt of bleached white sand that is Sanna Bay. From here savour fantastic views across to the Small Isles, best enjoyed at sunset.

(O) Ardnamurchan, the most westerly point on the British mainland; (L) Ardnamurchan Lighthouse; (T) Sanna Bay; (B) Loch Sunart

Bealach na Bà

It's said that the Bealach na Bà (Pass of the Cattle) on the Applecross peninsula is the highest mountain pass in Britain, with an ascent that rises 2054ft from almost sea level. At any rate, it's certainly the most spectacular. Approaching from Tornapress, just north of Lake Kishorn – where signs ominously warn against driving the route in larger vehicles – the road begins in fairly routine fashion. Then the gradient suddenly increases (it reaches twenty percent at its steepest section) and the curves become ever more sinuous, sculpted by a series of dramatic hairpin bends, all the while shadowed by an almighty tower of rock. For the truly fit, and possibly foolish, there's only one way to tackle the pass and that's by bike; indeed, the ascent is frequently rated as the toughest climb in Britain. However you decide to make the trip, the views at the top (2054ft) are simply stunning. On a clear day, spectacular panoramas stretch across to Skye and Raasay. Once at the summit you can relax in the knowledge that it's all downhill from here, unless you've got to cycle all the way back from the other side, of course.

(L) Bealach na Bà passes over the Russell Burn river; (T) Bealach na Bà is thought to be the highest mountain pass in Britain; (B) Hiker in the snow

Cape Wrath

(T) The moody cape

Closer to Iceland than to London, the forebodingly named Cape Wrath at the northwestern tip of the Scottish mainland is the definition of remote. This is nature at is most elemental, the kind of place where you half-expect to see a Viking warship glide into view – the windswept promontory does, after all, take its name from the Norse word *hvarf*, meaning 'turning place'. The most satisfying way to get here – the only way, in fact, unless you take the foot-passenger ferry from Keoldale then a minibus for 14 miles – is on foot from Sandwood Bay (full-day hike). However you get here, the rewards are immense, from the lonesome lighthouse built by Robert Louis Stevenson to the highest sea cliffs in Britain. Incredible views sweep northeast to Orkney and west to the Outer Hebrides. If it's solitude you're after, then this wild place takes some beating.

Eilean Shona

You might have been to Scotland's northwest Highlands before, but there really is nothing to compare to Eilean Shona. It's a private, car-free island; a tidal Loch Moidart skerry cast off the Ardnamurchan peninsula, but a place more akin to a lost world of adventures where the stag-topped hills are bordered by Indian Ocean-esque beaches. *Peter Pan* author J.M. Barrie holidayed here – prompting plenty of hat tips to Neverland – and the sense of having a Lost Boys caper is palpable. There is wild swimming and crabbing off the pontoon, but also eagle-watching, seal-spotting, hill-climbing, kayaking, picnicking, campfire-building, and art classes. Ask the island stewards and they'll happily give you a quad-bike tour along a coast framed by fudgy sands and cornflower-blue seas. Even more appealing are the island's nine secluded, self-catering Hebridean cottages, all of which are scattered to every point of the compass.

(O) Hiking country; (L) Tioram Cottage is set right on the shorefront of Loch Moidart; (T) Bedroom at The Bothy

Great North Trail

The UK's most exciting long-distance cycle route may begin in the Peak District but the greater length of its itinerary lies in Scotland, running from Kielder Forest by the border all the way to Cape Wrath and John O'Groats. Launched in 2019, the Great North Trail is groundbreaking in that it plots an almost entirely off-main-road course. In fact, the route ingeniously avoids traffic for the most part, instead taking in rough hill paths, disused railway lines, drove roads, old military roads, city cycle paths and canal towpaths as well as minor and single-track roads. Sure, this entails the occasional doubling back on yourself, but it neatly swerves the dread of A-roads up ahead, with only fresh air, wildlife and stunning scenery for company. The trail is a great, eco-friendly way to traverse the country and you'll be rewarded with a saddle's-eye view of the landscape as it peaks and troughs across the Borders, Central Belt and Highlands. It even skirts the city centres of Edinburgh and Glasgow. Some of the northerly sections can be challenging, but each stretch is colour-coded for difficulty via the MTB Trail Grading System so there are no nasty surprises.

(L) The trail takes in the undulating landscape of the Highlands

Smoo Cave

A mile east of Durness is Smoo Cave, a gaping hole in a limestone cliff created by the sea and a small burn. Tucked at the end of a narrow cove, the main chamber is accessible via steps. The rock formations are quite impressive, and if the weather behaves you can take a fantastic 20-minute tour that is partly by rubber dinghy into two further caverns; after heavy rain a waterfall cascades through the middle. Nearby, the white sands of Balnakeil Bay are stunning in any weather, but especially spectacular when sunny days turn the sea a Mediterranean turquoise. A path winds through the dunes behind to Faraid Head – fine views east to Loch Eriboll and west to Cape Wrath make this circuit (3–4hr) the best in the area. While here, drop by the Balnakeil Craft Village, a hippie commune borne out of a disused 1970s military camp.

(L) Covered wooden bridge leading into the limestone Smoo Cave; (T) Sango Sands;
(B) After heavy rain, a waterfall cascades through the cave

Inverewe Garden & Wester Ross

Inverewe Garden works best as a kind of palate-cleanser for Wester Ross – a soft, curated interlude in a region better known for raw nature. This is the stretch of the northwest Highlands where the scenery does all the heavy lifting: fjord-like sea lochs, a coastline scalloped by white-sand beaches and shattered cliffs, and mountains rising straight from the shoreline, with Skye and the Western Isles often hanging on the horizon in clear light. Then, tucked into this big, weather-made landscape, Inverewe offers a different register: sheltered paths, deliberate planting and a sense of calm that feels almost mischievous against the elements outside the garden gates. Come on a day when Atlantic fronts are doing their usual quick-change act and you'll get the full effect – sunshine one minute, squalls the next, everything freshly rinsed and bright. Slow down, let the weather pass, and enjoy the contrast.

(O) Inverewe Gardens, one of the most northerly botanical gardens in the world; (L) Rhododendrons along the path at Inverewe Gardens; (T) Loch Ewe viewed across the Walled Garden

Assynt & Suilven

(T) The glacial landscape of Inverpolly in Assynt

Assynt and Inverpolly don't ease you in. This is a landscape of lochans, bare rock and improbable mountains rising clean from a rough, empty spread – scenery that demands you slow the car. Suilven is the obvious scene-stealer, a singular ridge with a sugarloaf profile that seems almost sketched onto the skyline; catch sight of it from the road and a detour suddenly feels non-negotiable. Walkers come for the long approach across peat and stone, with a summit view that opens over scattered water, fractured rock and hills set apart like islands. Inverpolly adds to the strangeness: a wild jumble of moor, loch and mountain where Stac Pollaidh, Cùl Mòr and Cùl Beag give the horizon a jagged rhythm. The light can turn the hills silver in minutes, storms sweep through fast, and the silences are big enough to make a passing car feel notable. Nothing here feels tidied up for visitors. It is Scotland's ancient geology left exposed, dramatic and completely in charge.

Loch Maree & Slioch

Loch Maree holds the eye for even longer than most Highland lochs, thanks to its dark water, pine-fringed shores, bare rock and the scatter of islands breaking the surface. Above the northern shore, Slioch gives the scene its anchor – a clean, commanding mountain shape that pulls every view towards it. In calm weather the loch throws the hills back at themselves; in wind it darkens, roughens and feels more remote. This is a place for unhurried exploration, taking in roadside viewpoints, short shoreline walks and longer days in the hills. Strong walkers head for Slioch, a steep, demanding climb with a summit view over water, rock and the wider northwest Highlands. Others stay lower, watching the loch edge for movement and the sky for raptors. The reward is not spectacle at speed, but the slow build of a landscape that keeps revealing more the longer you stay.

(O) Loch Maree; (L) Wildlife spotting on the shore; (T) Cottage and boat; (B) Slioch

Glen Affric

Glen Affric has the rare ability to feel both welcoming and truly wild. The road ends, the crowds thin, and suddenly you're in a glen of lochs, rivers and surviving fragments of Caledonian forest, with hills rising in long, muscular slopes on either side. Walks here suit almost any level, from easy circuits by the water to longer routes that push deeper into the glen and up onto viewpoints where the landscape opens out in layers. Scots pines lean into the wind while reflections ripple across dark water, while that clean Highland air makes everything look sharper. It's also a reminder that Scotland isn't only about bare rock and heather – woodland has its own drama, especially when it's ancient and hardy. Once you're in Glen Affric, the main temptation is simply to get out on foot and keep going. Strong walkers head for the higher ground: steady climbs to viewpoints that give you that classic Affric reveal of lochs stitched through forest, then hills stacked behind. It's also ideal for quiet wildlife-watching in the trees – deer in the clearings and birds flitting through the pines.

(L) Rainbow over Glen Affric; (T) Autumn colours at Loch Affric; (B) The walk to Plodda Falls

Plockton

Plockton offers the epitome of Highlands charm without losing its edge. Sheltered by the curve of the coast and backed by hills, the village gathers around a pretty bay where boats bob on calm water that often looks more Mediterranean than north Atlantic, especially when the light is kind. That mild microclimate shows up in the palms and lush greenery, which adds to the pleasant sense of surprise. Yet it is still indisputably the real Highlands with its working harbour energy and sea air – and the constant presence of weather waiting offshore. Plockton sees many visitors as it easily it fits into a wider journey – a pause on the way to Skye, a base for short cruises or coastal walks, or simply an excuse to slow down and watch the day change over the water. It's photogenic without trying, and that's half the point.

(L) Plockton

Eilean Donan Castle

(T) The Castle at sunset

Eilean Donan is the castle everyone thinks they've seen before they've even arrived – and then you round the bend and realise the setting is even better in real life. Perched where sea lochs meet, with mountains rising behind, it looks engineered for maximum drama: water, stone, sky and a causeway that makes the approach feel appropriately ceremonial. It's a classic Scottish icon for a reason, but it doesn't feel tired. Weather transforms the setting from romantic to forbidding in minutes, and the light can turn the whole scene into a study in greys and silvers. The castle's popularity is easy to escape if you time it well, and it rewards those quieter moments when the tour-bus buzz fades and you're left with the simple power of the location. It's also a great "first taste of the west" stop: a quick hit of Highland drama before you push on towards Skye, Kintail or the empty road ahead.

Dunnet Head

Dunnet Head has the thrill of an endpoint, a place where the road and the land both seem to run out and the sea takes over. Often described as the true northern tip of mainland Britain, it delivers exactly what visitors come for: raw cliffs, broad skies and views that pull your attention out across the Pentland Firth towards Orkney. The headland feels exposed in the best possible way, with wind strong enough to sharpen your senses and make every step feel brisk. In summer the cliffs can be busy with seabirds – bring binoculars – and even outside the season, there's usually something looping, diving or riding the updrafts, not to mention the constant sense of movement from the waves, clouds and shifting light. Most people come for the big sky and big cliff drop-offs, but it's also a fine reset button after long drives, offering a few miles of air, space and salt, then back to the road with a clear head.

(L) Dunnet Head Lighthouse looking over towards the Island of Hoy; (T) The cliffs;
(B) The most northernly point of mainland Scotland

Skye & THE Small Isles

For many, Skye is the Highlands in miniature, comprised of shapely summits and shifting seascapes, superb hiking, wildlife and crofting villages, with classic Highlands weather thrown in for good measure. Often dubbed the Island of Mist, Skye rewards those who dodge the summer crush and roam into quieter corners. Just south, the Small Isles – Rùm, Eigg, Muck and Canna – may get only a trickle of the visitors, but still offer their own little escapes.

THE Cuillin

Sculpted by glaciers some 60 million years ago, The Cuillin was once a colossal volcano. Today, when the spectacular peaks aren't cloaked in mist, they dominate the Isle of Skye. Home to all the Munros on the island, the razor-edge mountain range includes the Black Cuillin, so-called for the colour of their coarse-grained jagged gabbro, and the gentler, rounded Red Cuillin, with picturesque Glen Sligachan between the two. Accessible viewpoints include Glenbrittle Campsite & Café, Sligachan village and the jaw-dropping boat trip from Elgol to Loch Coruisk. Hillwalkers and technical climbers get a lot closer to the action. Though none of the Munros are easily bagged, Bruach na Frìthe (3143ft), accessed via the Fairy Pools near Glenbrittle and Sgurr a' Fionn Choire, is the most straightforward. Not surprisingly, the menacing-sounding Inaccessible Pinnacle atop Sgùrr Dearg is generally considered the toughest.

(L) Loch Coruisk and the Cuillin from Sgurr na Stri; (T) The Cuillin was sculpted by glaciers; (B) Hiking the range

Eigg

(T) An Sgùrr

Eigg – which measures just five miles by three – does little to conceal its volcanic origins. It is made of a basalt plateau, and a great stump of pitchstone lava, known as An Sgùrr, rises in the south. Geology aside, Eigg has an appealingly strong sense of community among its 100-odd residents. This was given a boost in 1997 when they (alongside the Scottish Wildlife Trust) pulled off the first buyout of a Highlands estate, thereby ending Eigg's unhappy history of private ownership. The anniversary is celebrated with an all-night ceilidh on the weekend nearest June 12. Its other world-first is that its electricity grid is powered entirely by renewable sources. For visitors, the allure lies in scenic hikes, superb sea views and atmospheric crofting ruins. At low tide, scramble along the shore into Cathedral Cave or Massacre Cave (Uamh Fhraing), where all but one of Eigg's 396 inhabitants died in 1577, suffocated by the MacLeods of Skye, who lit a fire in the cave mouth.

Fairy Pools

One route into the mighty Cuillin is from Glenbrittle on the west side. The valley edges the most spectacular peaks, a semicircle of mountains which ring Loch Coruisk, before it runs to a beach at Loch Brittle. One of the least demanding walks is a five-mile round trip (3hr) from Glenbrittle campsite up Coire Làgan to a lochan squeezed among stern rock faces. An equally good reason to come is the Fairy Pools, one of Britain's most celebrated wild swimming destinations. There is no denying their beauty: sculpted rock pools filled with crystal-clear mountain spring water fed by a series of waterfalls. The scenery is superb as the river tumbles beneath peaks – the downside is icy water temperature of ten degrees Celsius at best, and its popularity is such that in summer months tailbacks of cars have been known to extend for miles along the single-track road. The pools are signposted from Glumagan Na Sithichean car park. The largest waterfall is a 2.4km walk from the car park, or continue on to discover a string of smaller pools.

(O) Tracing the mountain streams that feed the Fairy Pools; (L) Wildflowers flank the pools; (T) The rock pools are filled with crystal-clear mountain spring water; (B) Hiking past the Fairy Pools

Muck

Seen from southern Skye or the west coast of the Highlands, the Small Isles – Rùm, Eigg, Muck and dinky Canna – lie scattered in a silver-grey sea like a siren call to adventure. Barely two miles long, Muck is the smallest and most southerly of the archipelago. Its name derives from *muc*, the Gaelic for "pig" (or possibly *muc mara*, "sea pig" or porpoise, which are plentiful), and has long caused embarrassment to lairds – they preferred to call it the "Isle of Monk" because it briefly belonged to the medieval church. Port Mór is the hub of all activity, where just about all of the thirty or so residents live – a tenth of the 320 of the early 1800s. A mile-long road connects Port Mór with the island's main farm, Gallanach, which overlooks rocky skerries. The nicest sandy beach is Camas na Cairidh, to the east of Gallanach. For a stiffer challenge, Beinn Airein is worth climbing, despite being only 450ft above sea level, for a 360-degree panorama of surrounding islands from its summit. You can wild camp on the island or hole up in the Isle of Muck bunkhouse.

(L) Misty Muck

Rùm

After almost a century as the "Forbidden Isle" – the exclusive sporting estate of self-made Lancastrian industrialists the Bulloughs – Rùm has opened up. Many come to hike the eight-mile Rùm Cuillin Ridge Walk, tracking a crown of peaks that are modest by Skye's standards – the summit of Askival is only 2663ft – but every bit as impressive in looks. The island is renowned for its Manx shearwaters, which nest in burrows on high peaks. The best beach is Kilmory in the north, a flattish 10-mile walk on tracks through Kinloch then Kilmory glens. Most day-trippers to Rùm head straight for Kinloch Castle, a squat, red-sandstone edifice with decadent Edwardian interiors. It's also appealingly bonkers, packed with technical gizmos accumulated by Sir George Bullough (1870–1939), a spendthrift son. Visitors are permitted to wild camp, or take your pick from two simple bothies, a campsite, one bunkhouse or the island's first B&B.

(O) Rùm's form at sunrise; (L) White-tailed sea eagle; (T) Rùm's highest mountain, Askival

Sleat

The Sleat peninsula is unlike almost anywhere else on the Isle of Skye. An uncharacteristically fertile area, this southern corner of the island has been branded "The Garden of Skye". The main attraction is the Armadale Castle estate, but in 2017, the Talisker Distillery at Torabhaig opened, and tours and whisky tastings have since proved a hit. Scotland's most-touted island is the last place you'd expect to find a secret backcountry experience, yet look hard enough and Skye's Atlantic-facing sea lochs and islands remain a blank space for stand-up paddle boarding and sea-kayaking adventures. Set off from the beach at Ord across Loch Eishort, paddle to Coral Island, and then complete a wild camping circuit on Elgol by finishing back across the strait at Tokavaig. For a long day's paddle, embark from Armadale Castle to the isle of Ornsay, where you can splurge on a Michelin-starred dinner at Kinloch Lodge overlooking the Sound of Sleat.

(L) Kayak tour; (T) Kinloch Lodge; (B) Torabhaig Distillery

Old Man of Storr & the Quiraing

Trotternish is where Skye stops looking like just an island and starts resembling a myth. The Old Man of Storr rises from the ridge like a fossilised giant, a jagged pillar that turns every weather change into a new photograph, especially when the light drops towards sunset. It's especially good towards sunset, when the whole ridge starts to look theatrical. Nearby, the Quiraing is stranger still, a landslip landscape of cliffs, craters and basalt pinnacles, with walking trails that thread through scenery that feels half natural, half imagined. You can take it in by road on a loop from Portree, but it is on foot that the peninsula makes its case, when the wind catches your jacket and the views open over sea and moor. The walking trails are well marked, but the real fun is in taking your time: follow the path through the weird, landslip-sculpted terrain, then keep pausing to poke up little side rises for better angles on the cliff. Come early, before the car parks fill, and while the place retains its most otherworldly Skye magic.

(O) The Old Man of Storr; (L) Bride's Veil waterfall near the Old Man of Storr; (T) Hike amongst the heather; (B) Trotternish Ridge at sunset

THE Western Isles

Beyond Skye, across the unpredictable waters of the Minch, the Outer Hebrides – the Western Isles – stretch for 130 miles like a broken chain, wild and windy, with Atlantic surf on one side and a thousand sheltered bays on the other. Interiors flip from treeless peat moor to bare hills above lochans, while beaches of machair and pale sand feel almost unreal in clear light. It's Gaelic heartland, crofting country, and a proper edge-of-the-map escape.

Barra

Four miles wide and eight long, Barra is the Western Isles in miniature: sandy beaches, mountains of Lewisian gneiss – the oldest rock in Britain – prehistoric ruins and a Gaelic culture. A kind of feudal island state, it was ruled over for centuries by the MacNeils. Unfortunately, the family sold the island in 1838 to Colonel Gordon of Cluny, who deemed the starving crofters "redundant" and proceeded with some of the cruellest forced Clearances in the Hebrides. In 1937, the 45th chief of the MacNeil clan bought back most of the island, and in 2003 the estate was gifted to the Scottish government. At the island's southern tip, Castlebay – as its name suggests – has a castle in its bay: the picturesque medieval islet-fortress of Caisteal Chiosmuil, or Kisimul Castle, ancestral home of the MacNeil clan. To the west are the fine sandy beaches of Halaman Bay and Allasdale (Allathasdal), while rocky bays bite into the east coast. Further north, Barra is squeezed between two sandy bays: one of which – Tràigh Mhòr, or Cockle Strand – is also used as the island's airport runway at low tide.

(L) Tangasdale beach; (T) Barra Airport, Traigh Mhor beach; (B) Sea kayaking over clear water

Lewis & Harris

The most northerly of the Outer Hebrides (Western Isles), Lewis and Harris is, despite the name, just one island. Lewis (Leodhas) in the north is home to the Hebrides' main town of Stornaway and the Museum nan Eilean, with its famous twelfth-century chess pieces carved in Norway, as well as the Calanais Standing Stones that predate England's Stonehenge. Culture aside, most people visit Lewis and Harris for the dramatic landscapes, empty beaches, wild moorland and scenic lochs. The ruggedly beautiful mountains of North Harris are latticed with peaceful trails, and beyond tiny Tarbert, which links North and South Harris, it's all machair-strewn grassy plains and pearly white shell beaches. Stunning Luskentyre Beach, with its jewel-blue sea and rolling dunes, is unmissable.

(O) The beach at Luskentyre, Isle of Harris; (L) The Lewis Chessmen in Lews Castle Museum; (T) The Calanais Standing Stones predate England's Stonehenge

St Kilda

(T) Stac Lee, which at 544 ft is the second highest sea stack in the UK

Britain's westernmost island chain is the St Kilda archipelago, forty miles from North Uist. Dominated by Britain's highest cliffs and sea stacks, Hirta, the main island, was occupied until 1930 when the last 36 Gaelic-speaking inhabitants were evacuated at their own request. The Marquess of Bute then bought the island to protect the millions of nesting seabirds. In 1957, having allowed the army to build a missile-tracking radar station here linked to South Uist, the marquess bequeathed the island to the National Trust for Scotland (NTS). St Kilda is one of only two-dozen UNESCO World Heritage Sites with a dual status reflecting its natural and cultural significance. Despite its inaccessibility, several thousand visitors make it out here each year; if you get to land, you can see the museum, send a postcard and take in the glorious views. Between May and August, the NTS organizes volunteer parties to restore and maintain the old buildings or take part in archeological digs.

North Uist

Compared to the mountainous scenery of Harris, North Uist – seventeen miles long and thirteen miles wide – is much flatter than its popular neighbour. Over half the surface area is covered by water, creating a distinctive peaty-brown lochan-studded "drowned landscape". Most visitors come here for the trout- and salmon-fishing and the deerstalking, all of which (along with poaching) are critical to the survival of the island's economy. Others come for the smattering of prehistoric sites, the birds, the otters, or the sheer peace of this windy isle and the solitude of North Uist's vast sandy beaches, which extend – almost without interruption – along the north and west coasts. Base yourself in sleepy Lochmaddy to explore the cluster of prehistoric sites nearby. The only other thing to keep you in the port town is Taigh Chearsabhagh, a converted eighteenth-century merchant's house, now home to a community arts centre, with an airy café, shop and excellent museum, which puts on some worthwhile exhibitions.

(L) Lochmaddy village; (T) Scolpaig Tower, a Georgian folly; (B) The "drowned landscape" of North Uist

South Uist

South Uist is the largest and most varied of the southern chain of islands. The west coast boasts some of the region's finest machair and beaches – a necklace of gold and grey sand strung twenty miles from one end to the other – while the east coast features a ridge of high mountains rising to 2034ft at Beinn Mhòr. One of the best places to reach the sandy shoreline is at Howmore (Tobha Mòr), a pretty little crofting settlement with a number of restored houses, many still thatched, including one distinctively roofed in brown heather. It's an easy walk from the village church across the flower-strewn machair to the gorgeous beach. In among the crofts are the shattered, lichen-encrusted remains of no fewer than four medieval churches and chapels, and a burial ground now harbouring just a few scattered graves.

(L) South Uist boasts some of the region's finest beaches

SWAN
LK.243.

Orkney & Shetland

Orkney and Shetland sit out on Scotland's northern edge, fiercely distinctive and windswept, with a pull that feels almost Scandinavian. Orkney is a low-lying archipelago of big skies, Neolithic wonders and salty coastal walks, where locals proudly fly their own flag and call their largest island 'the Mainland'. Shetland lies further still, beyond the horizon – a place of sea-cliffs, crofting grit and summer "simmer dim", where weather and light set the mood.

GBR
3270T

Fair Isle

Marooned in the sea halfway between Shetland and Orkney, Fair Isle is very different from both. The weather reflects its isolated position: you can almost guarantee that it'll be windy, though if you're lucky your visit might coincide with fine weather – what the islanders call "a given day". The magical little island is bookended by a pair of a lighthouses, with a world-famous bird observatory in the middle. Fair Isle's population tumbled from 400 to 44 by the 1950s, at which point evacuation was seriously considered. The laird, George Waterston, who'd set up a bird observatory in 1948, passed it into the care of the National Trust for Scotland in 1954 and rejuvenation began. Today, Fair Isle supports a community of around sixty. The north end of the island rises like a wall, while the Sheep Rock, a sculpted stack of rock and grass on the east side, is another dramatic feature. Fair Isle's two lighthouses, one at either end of the island, are both designed by the Stevenson family and were erected in 1892 – the South Lighthouse can be visited by appointment.

(L, T) Fair Isle, marooned in the sea between Shetland and Orkney; (B) Atlantic puffin silhouetted at sunset on Fair Isle

Isle of Noss

Appropriately enough for an island that slopes gently into the sea at its western end, and plunges vertically 500ft at its eastern end, Noss has the dramatic and distinctive outline of a half-sunk ocean liner, while its name means "a point of rock". Inhabited until World War II, it's now a nature reserve and sheep farm, managed by Scottish Natural Heritage, who operate a RIB ferry from Bressay. An old farmhouse contains a small visitor centre, where the warden will give you a quick briefing and a free map. Nearby is a sandy beach, while behind the *haa* (laird's house) is a Pony Pund, a square stone enclosure built for the breeding of Shetland ponies. The most memorable feature of Noss is its eastern sea cliffs, rising to a 500ft peak at Noup, home to vast colonies of cliff-nesting gannets, puffins, guillemots, shags, razorbills and fulmars. As Noss is only a mile or so wide, it's easy enough to walk to the sea cliffs and back, but keep close to the coast, since otherwise the great skuas (locally known as "bonxies") may well dive-bomb you.

(O) Noss has the distinctive outline of a half-sunk ocean liner; (L) Northern gannet; (T) Cliffs plunge 500ft into the sea at the eastern tip of Noss; (B) Great skua seabird

Jarlshof

(T) View over the site

Of all the archeological sites in Shetland, Jarlshof is the largest and most impressive. What makes Jarlshof so amazing is the fact that you can walk right into a house built 1600 years ago, which is still intact to above head height. The name – misleading, as it is not primarily a Viking site – was coined by Sir Walter Scott, who used the ruins of the Old House in his novel *The Pirate*. However, it was only at the end of the nineteenth century that the Bronze Age, Iron Age and Viking settlements you see now were discovered, after a violent storm ripped off the top layer of turf. Only half of the original broch survives, and its courtyard is now an Iron Age aisled roundhouse, with stone piers. Inland lies the maze of grass-topped foundations marking out the Viking longhouses, from the ninth century AD. Towering over the whole complex are the ruins of the laird's house, built by Robert Stewart, Earl of Orkney and Lord of Shetland, in the late sixteenth century, and the Old House of Sumburgh, built by his son, Earl Patrick.

North Ronaldsay

North Ronaldsay – or "North Ron" as it's fondly known – is Orkney's most northerly island, with a population of around fifty. Separated from Sanday by some treacherous waters, it has an outpost atmosphere, brought about by its extreme isolation. Measuring just three miles by one, and rising only 66ft above sea level, the only features to interrupt the flat horizon are Holland House – built by the Traill family, who bought the island in 1727 – and a pair of lighthouses at Dennis Head. The island's most frequent visitors are ornithologists, who come to clock the rare migrants that land here briefly on their spring and autumn migrations. The attractive, stone-built Old Beacon lighthouse was first lit in 1789, but the lantern was replaced by the current huge bauble of masonry in 1809. The New Lighthouse, designed by Alan Stevenson in 1854, is Britain's tallest land-based one, at over 100ft. Climb the 176 steps to the top and admire the view.

(O) The empty shoreline of isolated North Ronaldsay;
(L) Local sheep are noted for their seaweed diet;
(T) Sunset from North Ronaldsay Lighthouse

Skara Brae

Lots of great stories start with a storm, and the discovery of the Neolithic homes at Skara Brae was thanks to an 1850 squall that blew away the sand dunes that for centuries had hidden this magical cluster of stone houses. Older than Stonehenge or the Great Pyramids, Skara Brae is a mesmerizing Neolithic settlement, crammed with domestic detail. Dating back 5000 years, the houses are incredibly well preserved, with narrow connecting passageways which would once have been covered with turf. Each home consists of a single living room, where stone cupboards, beds, boxes and fireplaces all survive to give a miraculous sense of early domestic life. It's thought that the inhabitants were some of Britain's earliest farmers: they grew wheat crops and raised pigs, sheep and cows. No weapons were found, indicating that life was peaceful here; what archeologists did discover were needles, jewellery, ceramics, buttons and dice, all suggestive of a creative, settled community.

(L, T, B) Skara Brae brings a Neolithic settlement to life in its well-preserved houses

Sumburgh Head

Shetland's South Mainland is a long, thin finger of land, only three or four miles wide but 25 miles long, ending dramatically in Sumburgh Head (262ft). The road up to the vertical cliffs is the perfect site for watching nesting seabirds such as kittiwakes, fulmars, shags, razorbills and guillemots, as well as gannets nosediving for fish. This is also the easiest place in Shetland to get close to puffins: during the nesting season (May to early Aug), you simply need to look over the wall as you enter the lighthouse complex to see them in their burrows a few yards below with beaks full of sand eels. Visit the clifftop lighthouse, built by Robert Stevenson in 1821, and explore some of the outbuildings, including the reconstructed World War II secret radar hut which helped protect the Royal Navy anchored in Scapa Flow. After roaming the complex, settle down and enjoy the sea views from the lighthouse's café.

(L) View towards the radar station

Ring OF Brodgar

One of Orkney's most iconic sights, the Ring of Brodgar is an enormous circle composed of thirty-six upright stones, some of them nearly five metres tall. Its precise age is unknown, but archeologists' best guesses suggest that it was erected about 4500 years ago. The 104m-wide circle is ringed by a ditch, or henge, and must have taken a phenomenal amount of work to complete, especially since some of the stones were probably brought here from quarries over six miles away. Set on a finger of land between the lochs of Stenness and Harray, it's a striking, sometimes haunting, place. Besides the Ring itself, there are a couple of other archeological sites here, including two mounds that may have been tombs, and – a short distance to the south – the Comet Stone, which stands alone outside the circle. It's unknown what its purpose was, but it may have been a marker for a path leading from the Ring of Brodgar to the Stones of Stenness.

(L) Stone at sunset; (T) Summer at the ring; (B) The stones are situated between the Loch of Stenness and the Loch of Harray

Publishing information

Scotland • 100 Legendary Places
Editor: Sarah Clark
Designer: Michał Ptasznik
Picture Manager: Tom Smyth
Production Operations Manager: Katie Bennett
Publishing Technology Manager: Rebeka Davies
Head of Publishing: Sarah Clark

Our selection

Scotland • 100 Legendary Places offers our curation of the most exceptional destinations in the country, with content drawn from *Rough Guides Scotland* and *100 Best Places in Scotland*, originally edited by Joanna Reeves. Contributors to these books included: Greg Dickinson, Brendan Griffin, Rob Humphreys, Norm Longley, Rachel Mills, Keith Munro, Joanna Reeves and Helena Smith.

First Edition 2026

ISBN: 9781835296462

Printed by Finidr in Czech Republic

MIX
Paper | Supporting responsible forestry
FSC® C014138

A catalogue record for this book is available from the British Library.

Distribution
UK, Ireland and Europe
Apa Publications (UK) Ltd; mail@roughguides.com
United States and Canada
Two Rivers; ips@ ingramcontent.com
Australia and New Zealand
Woodslane; info@woodslane.com.au
Worldwide
Apa Publications (UK) Ltd; mail@roughguides.com

Special Sales, Content Licensing and CoPublishing
Rough Guides can be purchased in bulk quantities at discounted prices. We can create special editions, personalized jackets and corporate imprints tailored to your needs.
mail@roughguides.com; http://roughguides.com

EU Representative
LOGOS EUROPE, 9 rue Nicolas Poussin, 17000, LA ROCHELLE, France
Contact@logoseurope.eu; +33 (0) 667937378

Caption key
(L) = left
(R) = right
(T) = top
(B) = bottom
(O) = opposite

Photo credits

Alamy 23T, 44, 45L, 45R, 76, 99T, 108, 124/125, 181L, 181R, 185BL, 196
Alexander Baxter 130/131
Alistair Edwards 175R
Ardoch Estate Loch Lomond 96
AWL Images 162/163
Courtesy of Jupiter Artland 16, 17L, 17R
Cycling UK/ Max Darkins 176/177
F Scholz/imageBROKER/Shutterstock 185TR
Fife Council/Damian Shields 118/119
FLPA/David Hosking/Shutterstock 80
Getty Images 51BR, 194
Glasgow Life 7CR, 64, 67B, 68/69, 70, 71BL, 71BR, 71TR, 72, 73R
Helen Cathcart 207T
Horst Friedrichs 207B
Ian Rutherford/Shutterstock 81T
Jack Brockway 174
Jane Barlow/Shutterstock 87B
Jonathan Perugia/Shutterstock 115TR
Liam Jones 175L
Lynn Bowser/Argaty Red Kites 98
Markus Keller/imageBROKER/Shutterstock 178
Michael Maehrlein/imageBROKER/Shutterstock 184
Mockford & Bonetti/Apa Publications 59T
Moor of Rannoch Restaurant & Rooms 138/139
National Museums Scotland 21BR
NorthLink Ferries 225T
Olaf Krüger/imageBROKER/Shutterstock 180
Peter McNally 161L, 161R
Philip Dunn/Shutterstock 172/173
Richard Elliot/VisitScotland 214
Robert Perry/EPA-EFE/Shutterstock 144
SG CIC Glasgow Museums Collections 67T
Shutterstock 8, 10/11, 12, 13B, 13T, 14/15, 19B, 21TR, 22, 23B, 30, 31T, 34/35, 36, 37B, 37T, 40/41, 46/47, 56, 57R, 60, 61BL, 61TR, 73L, 74, 77B, 79L, 81B, 82, 83BL, 83BR, 83TR, 86, 87T, 88, 89L, 89R, 90, 91B, 91T, 92/93, 94, 95BL, 95BR, 95TR, 99B, 102, 103R, 106, 107BL, 109B, 109T, 110/111, 114, 115BL, 115BR, 145L, 145R, 164, 165B, 165T, 168, 169BL, 169BR, 169TR, 170, 171B, 179T, 179B, 182/183, 185BR, 188/189, 192, 193T, 193B, 197B, 200, 201BL, 201BR, 201TR, 202/203, 204, 205L, 205R, 206, 208, 209BL, 209BR, 209TR, 216/217, 224, 225B, 227BL, 227BR, 227TR, 228/229, 232, 233B, 236, 237B, 237T
Sim Canetty-Clarke 149B, 149T
South of Scotland Destination Alliance/Duncan Ireland 32, 33BL, 49B
The Gleneagles Hotel 134, 135B, 135T
The Glenturret 136, 137T, 137B
The Prince's Foundation/Dumfries House 62/63
Vicky Brock 226
VisitScotland/Cutmedia 7TR
VisitScotland/Damian Shields 2/3, 7BL, 7TL, 38, 49T, 160
VisitScotland/David N Anderson 26, 28/29
VisitScotland/Ian Rutherford 33TR
VisitScotland/Jakub Iwanicki 152
VisitScotland/John Duncan 198/199
VisitScotland/Kenny Lam 0, 7BR, 18, 19T, 20, 21BL, 24/25, 31B, 33BR, 48, 50, 51BL, 51TR, 54/55, 57L, 58, 59B, 66, 77T, 84/85, 100/101, 103L, 104, 105B, 105T, 107BR, 107TR, 112, 116, 117B, 117T, 120, 121B, 121T, 122/123, 126, 127B, 127T, 128, 132, 133BL, 133BR, 133TR, 140, 143T, 148, 150/151, 154, 155BL, 155BR, 155TR, 156/157, 158, 159T, 166, 171T, 186, 187B, 187T, 190/191, 197T, 215L, 215R, 233T, 234/235, 241
VisitScotland/Luigi Di Pasquale 146/147, 159B
VisitScotland/Paul Tomkins 42, 43B, 43T, 52, 61BR, 78, 79R, 142, 210, 212, 213T, 213B, 218, 219B, 219T, 220/221, 222, 230, 231L, 231R
Vistit Scotland/Visit Aberdeenshire 143B

Cover credit: Loch Awe and Kilchurn Castle **iStock**

Scotland *is* **waiting**

Make the **legend** your own